INSPIRATION
FOR WRITERS
BY WRITERS

Compiled by
Kristen Joy Laidig & Natalie Marie Collins

gréine
PUBLICATIONS

CHAMBERSBURG, PA

Published by Gréine Publications in 2019

Chambersburg, Pennsylvania

First edition; First printing

Each chapter ©2019 by their respective authors.

Cover design by Kristen Joy Laidig

ISBN 978-1-941638-17-0

TO THOSE WHO LOOK FEAR IN
THE FACE AND WRITE ANYWAY.

TABLE OF CONTENTS

INTRODUCTION

KRISTEN JOY LAIDIG & NATALIE MARIE COLLINS

Writing is art. It seems so simple. And yet writing is much deeper than what we traditionally think of when we hear the word *art*. Writing is also a baring of the writer's soul. It is the ability to put the reader in a position where they can peer into the eyes of the author and feel the depth of emotion as they read the words. It's the expression of thoughts, concepts, feelings, discoveries, and exploration reaching across the endless expanse from one human's mind to another. It's the presentation of new ideas and persuasion to new ways of thinking.

It is, in its purest definition, the expression of a thought of more than ordinary significance. And yet in its simplest definition… Writing is *Art*.

Any writer will tell you that writing means more to them than the dictionary definition of "to compose and produce in words" or "to express ideas." Rather to them it is an expression of their innermost thoughts, desires, dreams, and fears. An expression which can rarely take any other form but that of words strung together into complex sentences, thoughts, and stories.

Most writers will tell you writing comes as naturally to them as breathing... and yet sometimes it's as foreign to them as the desert is to a whale. Ernest Hemingway described it best when he said, "There is nothing to writing. All you do is sit down at a typewriter and bleed." Hemingway described the fate of every writer. We bleed more than words, thoughts, ideas, and frustration. We writers bleed our very souls.

This book is filled with stories by writers like you who found their expression through the written word. The contributors are a blend of accomplished bloggers, article writers, published authors, novelists, and most of all those who simply *must* write.

They understand the terror of the blank page, the blinking cursor that mocks the aspiring author until letters appear as the writer vomits all over their blank canvas. They get that sinking feeling in the pit of the writer's stomach as they read over their messy rough drafts and wonder how they could ever be successful at this craft.

And they know what it takes to press through and keep pushing on toward their dreams through their soul-written words.

Because to them, to you, to us... there is no option but to write. It is a compulsion we obsess over until satisfied. And it is an addiction with no end. We are doomed to write. We are called to write. And we are honored to write.

Because we are writers.

When you're bleeding upon that blank page, pick up this book and read the inspiration within its pages. Take heart in their words. Feel their passion for your art. Breathe new life into your written creation. And remember, you are also called to write.

Because *you* are also a *writer*.

1

YOU HAVE PERMISSION

NATALIE MARIE COLLINS

Writing takes a lot of intense focus to really be able to get into "the zone."

What is "the zone" exactly?

For a writer, it's that space we crave to get to where the flow of creative ideas and words just stream through us. It's the space where we give ourselves permission to see and listen to what really wants to be said, what story wants to be told, and to see it come to life through our mind's eye first. It's also the space where the ego takes a step back and allows true brilliance to come to life.

The true brilliance that comes through the zone is what every writer strives for, yet it can also be elusive, as if it's a myth. But once you get a taste of it, it becomes a craving to get back there because that is the space where you can tap into your true potential.

The world we live in today has become a cesspool of advertisements and distractions specifically designed to keep you from focusing on your own potential. Instead, they keep you focusing and consuming someone else's potential or product that subconsciously tells you you're not enough. This leads to deep frustration because our potential gets pushed down and blocked out to make way for the constant barrage of things competing for our precious attention.

Don't believe the "not enough" lie.

Your job as a writer is to become ruthless with how you spend your time and attention. Who gets it and who doesn't. With yourself taking first priority. You get to make the choice of who has permission to distract you and who doesn't. You get to make your own schedule and decide how you spend your time. You also get to determine where you are going to write.

> YOUR JOB AS A WRITER IS TO BECOME RUTHLESS WITH HOW YOU SPEND YOUR TIME AND ATTENTION.

It's your job as the human vessel, the deliverer of messages and inspiration, to give yourself permission to create the space for the zone to happen. You are the protector and keeper of your time. It's up to you to create boundaries with your friends, family, work obligations—and especially yourself—to give yourself permission to do the work and to write.

There are a hundred and one different things that can and will pop up in an instant that will make you feel as if they are more important than your writing. These distractions are what you have to be ruthless with, cutting and blocking in order to make the space for the writing to come through you. And yet, as hard as you may try, if you're working from home, the distractions tend to just keep coming.

The cat wanting food? Of course.

Your spouse wanting to show you the latest funny cat video? Yep.

Your kid tormenting said hangry cat and crying when they get scratched? That too.

This is when shifting your surroundings can become incredibly beneficial. Whether that's locking yourself in a room and letting everyone know, including the cat, that you are not to be disturbed, or taking yourself on a Writing Date outside of the house. Somewhere like a coffee shop, a co-working office space, or even a nice cafe. Places where being around others is okay, but they are not going to bother you, and you also have no responsibilities nagging at you in your surroundings.

By changing your surroundings and knowing that your focus for your Writing Date is to actually give yourself permission to write, it will help you tap into the collective creativity. It also helps to change your brain-space to help you shift away from your everyday distractions and leave them where they belong, which opens up the space in your mind to allow focus to happen and creativity to flow.

Going to a coffeeshop is a great example of this. There are always others there doing their work, whether they are working, writing, or reading. When you are in that kind of environment, those around you become your silent accountability partners working alongside of you to get things done. There is a special energy that comes from a space where others are working that you can sink into and allow it to give you what you need to do your writing. When you're in this type of environment, it becomes natural to sink into the collective work energy.

If leaving your house isn't ideal or possible, or you need to be even more focused, you can join a group of writers who meet through an online space and write together. No training or interruptions, just connecting and working. Together. In silence.

Groups like the one found at WritingDate.com meet once a week for an hour, setting a timer and holding the space for everyone to set their goal and accomplish it in the allotted time span. Writers who join this group are always amazed with how focused they become and how much they are able to accomplish.

This online working space creates a type of parallel universe where you can work from wherever you're at around the world and connect with others from wherever they are, and you come together to create a space where you know everyone is working with you to get things done. Like what happens in a coffee shop.

There is another factor of what happens inside of a timed work setting: *time warps*. That's right. Time warps.

Goal setting is important because it creates what the accomplishment is and in what timeframe it needs to get accomplished. Time will either stretch or contract to fit inside of that set timeframe, therefore "warping" itself.

The last component to warping time is you and your solid faith and commitment to completing the goal in the set timeframe. For instance, have you ever had a project deadline you had to meet that gave you an unreasonably short amount of time to accomplish it? A deadline that seemed almost impossible to accomplish, yet you did it anyways? Your commitment to completing the project on time is what really made it all come together and time warp. Under these types of pressures, you naturally put up boundaries, create the space for yourself to get it done, and do it. You become ruthless with how you spend your time because your priority is finishing the project. No excuses.

> ALLOW YOURSELF TO FULLY GET IN THE ZONE, AND WRITE.

There's the flip side of this scenario as well. If you have ample amounts of time to complete a project, chances are time will expand and stretch out over the set completion timeframe. If you only have two hours to complete something, chances are you'll get it done in that timeframe. If you have two weeks to complete something, chances are you'll get it done in that timeframe too. Even if it's the exact same project that you could complete in the two-hour timeframe.

Same goes for your book. If you're in the middle of writing a book and have not given yourself a deadline of when you'll accomplish it, chances are it will never get done. Likewise, if you're not setting the space for yourself to accomplish your writing, like blocking it off in your calendar, locking yourself in your office, or taking yourself on a writing date, when will it actually get done? Chances are it won't.

You've been given the idea and your deep soul desire to write for a reason. Nobody will fully understand that reason, including yourself, until you sit down, block all distractions, focus on your work, allow yourself to fully get into the zone, and write.

- Write what you hear.
- Write what you see.
- Dictate the story that is unfolding for you when you close your eyes.
- Get curious about what's there.
- Ask questions.
- Take notes.
- Explore the possibilities.
- Let the potential unfold for you.
- Allow the brilliance of it all to come through and share it with the world.

Why? Because it's for you to see first, to marvel at and bring into the physical world. Then once it's in physical form, it'll be time to show it to others so they can also marvel in the beauty of what's come through.

To honor this, you must first give yourself permission to block out distractions.

- ✍ Permission to focus.
- ✍ Permission to do the work.
- ✍ Permission to get into the zone.
- ✍ Permission to see it.
- ✍ Permission to let the magic come through you.
- ✍ Permission to make it a reality.

If giving yourself permission is the hardest part (as it is for most), join a writing group like the one at WritingDate.com and let them hold the space for you and give you permission first to do the work you're here to do.

When others give you permission first, it's easier to give yourself permission and step into your potential.

You have permission to write.

You have permission.

Write.

ABOUT

NATALIE MARIE COLLINS

Natalie Marie Collins survived 13 years inside the corporate world. She knew there had to be a better way and figured out how to make a living by taking her office skills home and started working as a Virtual Assistant, learned the ropes of how to create membership areas, branding, marketing, digital products, sales funnels and so much more.

She now coaches others on how to build a solid online business by sharing her vast knowledge with others on how they can have an easier and better life through patterns and rhythms that work. She also helps others with the clarity they need in their business + life and practical, actionable steps to be able to move forward and create the business that is right for them.

She is also the creator of National Writing Date Day and now has weekly Writing Dates that holds the space for you to be productive and having fun doing it.

Visit NatalieMarieCollins.com to learn more.

2

WRITING CHALLENGE INSPIRATION

JESSE BUTLER

It's funny how I was determined to start writing and publishing to encourage kids to allow their creativity to be pushed, to never let it die down. I always tell my daughter how amazing it is that she has such a vivid imagination. She can play for hours upon hours by herself in her room. Whether she is playing with Barbies, babies, play dough or whatever, she has a whole backstory to everything and knows exactly what she wants and every day is different. I never want her to lose her imagination, her dreamland. She plays well with others, but I can see the dramatic difference between her play time alone and when friends join in. Her friends struggle with creativity. If they can't see it, it's not there. They don't dream things up. To me, it's like life, if you can't daydream of what you want and clearly see your vision, how will you ever get to it? What if your goal is to be a famous basketball player or business owner? If you put limitations on yourself because you cannot see yourself in that life, how will you ever get the life you want?

When I was younger, I made a children's book out of colored paper and cardboard. It was about a tiger. Looking back, it may have been a short story about Tigger the Tiger (he was my favorite Pooh character). I remember my mom—an elementary aide at the time, now elementary and school librarian—telling me I should be an author when I grew up, "there is a huge demand for children's book authors," she said.

I loved the idea of being an author. I thought, "What a glorious job that would be. I wouldn't have to go to work or clock in, and I could do whatever I wanted most days. When I do choose to write, it would just magically appear on the pages," or so I thought. We all wish, right? I also wanted to be a professional basketball player and a sports reporter. What a life, huh! Those interests are all so different, how could I be all of them?

I went to college for communication studies and interned as a sports reporter. It was awesome! However, when my mentor suggested a high-maintenance look that I was less than interested in pulling off, I became discouraged and decided sports reporting wasn't for me. Plus, if I was going to have a family one day, the schedule wouldn't work. I still believe that to a point. However, if I was still interested in being a sports reporter, I would utilize YouTube and be my own producer and then create my own sports blog. Why not? There is an opportunity!

Life took me in another direction. By the end of 2011, it brought me back to the idea of becoming an author. I had recently seen a free webinar on how to create children's books and thought, "I could do this."

I began creating children's books as a way to connect with my kids. I thought it would be fun to answer each of their problems or questions with a book, one that was specifically created for them. I got to thinking that this would be a great way to supplement my lack of income while on maternity leave. I've always been unrealistic with timeframes, that's probably why I am either right on time without a moment to spare or the normal five to ten minutes late. I had no idea how long it would really take to start seeing success with my books. How could I? I was losing opportunities because I was missing half the information. I didn't realize that the maxim "if you build it, they will come" wasn't going to happen if no one knew "it" existed. Getting my books onto Amazon was one thing, one piece of the puzzle, but I needed to find all the pieces to make it work.

I wrote one children's book. Well, actually, one *Kindle* children's book. It was very poor quality (and I still need to fix it), but I did it! It was published in 2012 and didn't sell a copy for months. Again, discouraged, I started looking for some other way to supplement our income. Can you say "shiny object syndrome"? Yes, that was me.

I was infatuated with the idea of writing children's books, so I watched every free webinar on book creation, illustrations, writing, formatting and publishing. Do you know how many webinars and videos are out there? A lot. I'm pretty sure I saw most of them.

I watched them, but didn't follow through on the challenges to actually try what they suggested and to implement those steps. I had all these ideas and would start writing them out in note-books—lots of notebooks—but I never finished any of them. Sounds about right. I got started on something but never followed through. Now, who can I blame for that?

This time I blamed it on the fact that I had kids at home and needed to take care of them, and that my sister-in-law needed help with her own; so, now I had three kids, plus my house needed cleaning (like that happened with three kids under the age of four) and I needed to have dinner ready for my husband when he got home. Naturally, once he got home I didn't want to be working; I wanted to spend time with him. I may have had a few excuses and I just kept making more. Eventually, I went back to work and then I had a whole new set of excuses. I still wanted to create children's books, but never made it a priority.

I had proven my writing skills at work, which opened doors to new responsibilities that brought some creative fun into my daily grind. This led to a few contract opportunities. They were short-term, but gave me a chance to practice honing my writing skills.

I still had multiple idea journals and a stack of half used notebooks with incomplete stories in them. I went back to trying to complete the stories but instead continued to fill my idea journals with more and more book projects. It's funny how I can have a gazillion ideas but not finish any of them. Yeah, not so funny!

My son was taking karate lessons and he loved the idea of "publishing a book," so we created a picture book of his Shotokan moves. Wow, another rough-looking book. But he loved it. He had a huge sense of pride in what he created. This came at an opportune time. He was lacking confidence in his skills, but realized several of his classmates were struggling to remember any of the kata. He was able to create a picture book demonstrating each move, helping his classmates improve.

After recognizing the value of one child teaching another, I knew that encouraging kids to write and publish books would help other children overcome their own struggles. Something was still missing; I just wasn't quite sure what it was yet. So, I continued to dive deep into book publishing and how to increase sales.

IT WAS LIKE TRYING TO MAKE BREAD WITHOUT FLOUR.

I came across many more webinars during my research into book sales and discovered the missing ingredient. Honestly, it was like trying to make bread without flour. The most important step in becoming a successful author and I didn't even know I needed to do it. Now that I know about marketing and how it affects my book sales, I knew I needed to dive deeper and get creative.

I had started a YouTube channel reading children's books aloud thinking that it would eventually be a great way for me to market my books. My YouTube channel and Facebook page started getting a lot of views and several requests from other authors to read their books aloud. I was loving this! I'd get these free children's books in exchange for a YouTube video.

I *love* children's books. Anyone who knows me, knows I have a weakness for buying and reading kids' picture books. The teachers at my kids' school know that I am an easy sell when it comes to the Scholastics Book Club and I probably already registered for a dozen books before they even send the order form home. All the Usborne reps have tracked me down too. So, creating this *Reading Children's Books* YouTube channel was just a natural extension of my interests, a non-salesy way of marketing children's books for authors. However, I still needed to create my own children's books to try out my strategy.

During my time building an audience on my Facebook and YouTube channels, I had unpublished authors reaching out to me to help them publish their books. So, I started publishing children's books for "self-published" authors, kind of a ghost publisher for those who did not want to learn or had no idea where to start when publishing their books.

I began publishing their books for them and I started to see a huge improvement in my skills. The authors began getting sales. We updated covers and they saw another increase in sales. I was getting a rush from seeing my clients' work grow under my coaching. I had done so much research for my own benefit, that once I started implementing all the steps I had learned, in the right order, I was seeing results for my clients' work. I was laying out, formatting, and designing their books. Once they were published,

I would tell the authors what their next step should be, and as long as they followed through on it, they'd see results.

I FELT LIKE THERE HAD TO BE AN EASIER WAY.

This got me writing emails, texts and posts on how to prep your book, what the images need to be set at, and organizing the layout in order to get your book published. Between this and all the phone calls I got with the same questions, I felt like there had to be an easier way. So, I started making how-to videos and created a Build-Your-Book book that took others through the steps to quickly get their project started and move in the direction of being published. I am currently working on a course to better illustrate each step with demonstrations.

While publishing other authors' books, I created and published several journals, planners, and guides. I've discovered that even though I love to read children's books, my writing has evolved into the "how to", nonfiction genre for kids, teens, and adults. I love the idea of solving a problem for someone else by giving them all the tools and information I've learned along the way.

My writing has expanded from emails to individual clients, to blogs and articles reaching many. I have utilized my YouTube channels and combined my knowledge of publishing with my expertise in other industries to create valuable information, solving issues for an even wider audience. It feels good to see my value.

Being a writer isn't just about becoming a published author, having a dozen or so books associated with your name. Being a writer can mean being the spontaneous personality behind a brand, the creative mind behind the blog, or the marketing genius for an up-and-coming venture. Whether you are writing for your own benefit in a personal journal, creating playful phrases to share across twitter, or typing incessantly to finish a novel, you are a writer and you are creating art. Create for your own enjoyment or for others to enjoy.

I've grown to enjoy writing as a way to help others. I love to learn and implement what I've learned, and I like to keep trying new things. Creating how-to books gives me the opportunity for both. I get to expand my own understanding of anything from making cookbooks for kids, to helping long-haul truck drivers save money while on the road, to mindset hacks for youth athletics. I create books, videos, articles, guides, and checklists based on what I have learned and my interpretation, how it affects my life and how I see it helping others. By no means am I an expert in some of those fields, but I bring value to others by gathering details from multiple sources and summarizing them for easy reference.

I've discovered that if you really enjoy something and give yourself time to absorb it, then creating something from what you've learned can be wonderful, whether it be a story, an illustration or a video. That's why I write. That's why I create.

DON'T ALLOW PEOPLE TO PIGEONHOLE YOUR IDEAS.

It's art. It's my way of expressing how I feel, how I understand something, and helping others. Don't allow people to pigeonhole your ideas and tell you that their way or society's way of doing something is the only way.

In the last decade alone, hundreds or thousands of stories of individuals who have created something out of their passion when everyone else told them it couldn't be done or that no one would buy it. Share your imagination, show off your skills, and develop your thoughts into something you can own, develop, and identify with. That's art. And that's a life, right?

I thrive off of competition and don't even have to be competing against someone. It can be a challenge I've set for myself or the idea of excelling at something. You can't become good at something without practice, and oftentimes, you don't know what to practice if you don't understand what it is you're doing. You don't know what you don't know.

Do you ever have something pique your interest enough that you go searching for the answer only to discover that there is more than one answer out there? Or maybe find out that before you can truly understand the answer to your intriguing dilemma you must research further?

I find that out all the time and love it. I'm not necessarily frustrated with not immediately knowing the answer. It's like playing in a tournament; you are so excited to get to the end of each game just to see the outcome, yet you are enjoying the sport so much you don't want it to end. That's how I am with research, although I don't usually think of it as such, because if I did, that sounds too much like work (and I don't want to work), I want to relax and enjoy the experience. I just want to have fun.

Take marketing for example. I love the idea of marketing. It's challenging. It's creative. It's thought-provoking. It's multifaceted. There is so much to learn about your customers, their needs, their wants, their desires, and each can change depending on the subject they are being presented with. Then there is the product or service you are marketing. What does it do? What problems does it solve? How will someone benefit from it? Why would they want it? What about the company? What's their angle? How do they want to be represented? What are they the best at? What are their goals? Why are they doing what they are doing? This is the challenge.

There are hundreds of answers to those questions, but you have to engage in each of them to discover a unique sales position, the marketing angle that once done correctly, will attract customers or clients, increasing awareness and boosting sales. Marketing in a way that sets one brand ahead of and above others.

But how will you know how to do that? How will you know how to set this company, this brand, over and above its competitors? You won't; not until you start researching the market, their competitors, their strengths and weaknesses. You dig, you read, you research, you start asking questions, finding answers to some of them and then analyzing all the data you compiled. Breaking down possible aspects, discovering multiple angles to each distinguishing characteristic of The Brand versus the other companies. You create a proposition based on the evidence you collected and mold it into an undeniably superior brand in the eyes of the consumer. This generates enthusiasm around the uniqueness it provides. Buyers flock to have it or be part of its community all because you presented it to them in a way that made them long for it and feel they had to have it.

Marketing copy is an art form. Done right, it can create a fan of loyal followers. Done wrong, it will destroy your credibility.

Just as writing marketing copy can provide a vivid illustration of which protein drink best maximizes lean muscle growth for an amateur bodybuilder, writing a book that answers the who, what, where, why and how of a particular subject can be just as stimulating to those searching for solutions to their unanswered questions.

That's what I enjoy. It's what challenges me and creates an eagerness within me to know more. I love to read. Self-help, mindset, business management, inspirational and Christian living are some of my favorite genres. I like the idea of personal growth, and I get that from reading those. But growth doesn't stop at reading them; it continues by following through with what I have learned from those books. Whether I'm challenging myself to be a better Christian and show more compassion, or produce more content in my own style, I won't soar until I push myself beyond my own zone of comfort. It's like working out; you push yourself beyond the limits, tearing down your muscle just so you can build it up to be stronger and more efficient.

Writing allows me to be able to create something out of the written word that pushes others to act, to think, and to create something themselves, just as others have done for me. That's what writing is to me

There are some things and some people you just can't be better than in a particular arena, and that's ok. That doesn't stop me from trying. It just means I need to find another path to the basket. I'll excel using a different lane, finding my unique positioning and perfect it; show it to the world for those who were meant to read it. My dream is to influence others in my own way and encourage them just as other writers, have encouraged me to use writing to share my views and perspectives. I want to encourage aspiring authors to persevere and reach their goals no matter how competitive they feel the market is. There is no competition when it comes to being you. No one can be better at being you than you. Own it. Your story is waiting to be read too.

ABOUT

JESSE BUTLER

Jesse Butler takes a unique angle to book marketing, seeing the power of video firsthand. She is the author, creator, and publisher of *Market Research for Children's Book Publishing, My Daily Summer Journal series, Youth Athletics journal series, Wanting is Not Enough journal*, and *Win or Lose*. She is also the creator of the *Truckers 101* series, designed to get truck drivers the best tips and strategies in the industry to further improve their skills and attain success in their financial goals.

Jesse is also the publisher at Publishing Our Children's Stories, where she provides formatting, layout, cover design, and publishing services to independent authors looking to maintain their rights as sole owner of their children's books. In addition to her publishing services, she offers promotion services designed to catapult authors' book sales through video marketing.

Jesse is a wife, momma of two, and wannabe superhero. She and her family live in Montana with their dog, cat, ducks, Dragon, and fish. Jesse can usually be found attempting a low profile coaching gig covering several sports, canoodling with parents and teachers to strengthen their community, and trying many projects ideas with her kids.

Visit Facebook.com/learnfromreading to learn more.

3

WRITING INSPIRATION TIPS

KIM MARTIN

When I was a young girl, my mother taught me many practical things I would need later on in life to succeed. However, the one thing I am most grateful for is the love and joy of reading that she instilled in me by her own example. My mom was an avid reader, and as I was growing up she regularly took my younger sister and I to the local public library.

Later on as a teenager, and before I was old enough to drive, we lived close enough to the library that I was allowed to walk there by myself. When school was out for the summer I would fill a tote bag with books to read and kept myself busy all week long. Then I would go back and exchange them for new books. I repeated this cycle throughout my teenage years. I have vivid memories of getting lost in the stories I read, curled up on the lounge chair in our backyard, or lying on a blanket beneath an old weeping willow tree on the edge of a nearby farm.

My love of reading books as a child and teenager are what initially drew me to becoming a writer. Books are magical. I love being transported to another place or time. I love using my imagination to conjure up images of the scenes in every story I read. Time stands still for me when I read, and I find myself transforming into the characters I read about in so many books.

For that reason, I have a tremendous love for our public libraries. They have given me the free gift of an unending supply of books and magazines to read; some that have ignited my imagination, others that have provided an escape from my mundane life, and still others that have given me knowledge I desperately needed. Which leads me to:

WRITERS INSPIRATION TIP #1: READ A LOT

Read books, magazines, blogs, newspapers, and whatever interests you. Reading stimulates the imagination and teaches us about the human condition. Reading evokes our emotions, touches our hearts and inspires us. And, for more practical reasons, reading helps us improve our vocabulary and learn new words. Reading is a hands-on way to study the art of language without effort, and teaches us intuitively how to write.

Additionally, if you are a writer who is out of practice, facing writer's block, or has lost inspiration, reading can fuel your writing. Reading beckons us to fall back in love with writing and playing with words.

Growing up, one of my favorite authors was C. S. Lewis, who wrote the "Chronicles of Narnia" series. I was absolutely spellbound by *The Lion, The Witch and The Wardrobe*, a fantasy tale about good winning out over evil. I cried when Aslan, the lion, sacrificed his life to the White Witch in order to spare Edmund's life. Later on as a parent, it was fun to read his stories to my children, and in recent years I have enjoyed watching the movies adapted from his books.

In my early twenties, I was completely absorbed in reading romance novels set in the early 19th century of the British Regency. I became fascinated and drawn into the stories about the social activities of the fashionable young men and women considered to be members of high society. It was also enlightening to read about the differences among the social classes during that time period. My life was pretty boring, and reading about the social season of the British aristocrats and things like carriage rides, dinner parties, assemblies and balls seemed so romantic to me.

In my thirties I was riveted by stories about crime, especially if the protagonist was a woman. Two authors that I regularly read were Sarah Paretsky and Patricia Cornwell. I was particularly drawn into Patricia Cornwell's series featuring medical examiner Kay Scarpetta, and Sarah Paretsky's series about female bounty hunter V.I. Warshawski. I was attracted to both of these characters because they had careers in typically male-dominated positions. The characters made me believe that women are not limited to certain career fields and are competent to perform all types of work.

My all-time favorite author is Billie Letts. I discovered her when I watched the movie, *Where the Heart Is*, based on Letts book by the same title. It's an irresistible story about a homeless, pregnant 17-year-old girl who secretly lives in an Oklahoma Wal-Mart, where she meets genuine, caring people who help her turn her life around. I love the characters and story so much that I have read the book and watched the movie a few dozen times. To my dismay, Letts only had four published novels before she died in 2014.

While my reading tastes have changed over the years, what I enjoy most are stories about good winning over evil, overcoming adversity, and love conquering all. These are the stories that inspire me and give me courage and hope.

If there is a particular genre you want to write for, I strongly recommend you read oodles and oodles of those type of books, because it will help you absorb the ebbs and flows or the stylistic conventions found within that genre. There are also plenty of books and resources on the internet available to help you breakdown plot, as well as how, when, and where different aspects of your story should appear in your chosen genre.

Obviously, reading has been a big part of my life and has helped me gain a better sense of who I am and what matters to me. Everything you read will help you grow personally and as a writer.

WRITERS INSPIRATION TIP #2: WRITE A LOT AND WRITE DAILY!

Writing regularly builds your writing muscles. Remember, not everything you write has to be something you want to have published. For instance, you can keep a personal diary or a writing journal.

> WRITING REGULARLY BUILDS YOUR WRITING MUSCLES.

Over the years I have used both a diary and journal, and believe me when I say that getting your thoughts down on paper is very liberating and illuminating. When I read through my old journals I am inspired by how much I have grown as a person, and sometimes they give me ideas I can use later in my writing.

For example, in a diary or journal you can open up freely and explore any issues you struggle with or challenges you face, which can become fodder for your fictional characters. Writing in a journal helps me discover topics I am passionate about, or personal stories I can use to illustrate a point I want to make when I write a non-fiction piece.

I also keep an idea folder for non-fiction articles. It includes the thoughts or knowledge I have on a topic, sources of information, research, case studies, and personal stories, as well as quotes that resonate with me. Story journals are another useful place to keep ideas you have for your fiction. You can store your ideas either electronically on your computer or in physical folders and notebooks. I use both, but prefer the physical ones because I like to be able to touch and handle them.

Before I sit down to write, I try to prepare my environment. I may light a scented candle or listen to music that evokes a specific mood within me. Personally, I am more productive when I use a timer. I set it for twenty minutes. After the timer goes off I take a quick five minute break. During that time, I either get a drink or a snack, stretch my muscles, or go outside for some fresh air. Working in this way helps me absorb what I have written, and reflect on what else I want my reader to know about the topic.

I am a very pragmatic writer. Whenever I start an new article or blog post, I make a list of all the ideas and information I have about the topic. Then I put together an outline. Sometimes I put each idea on a separate sticky note to make it easier to see and organize all my ideas into categories and subcategories.

I try not to make any revisions until I have written most of the content. Then, while I am revising and editing I look for places where I can add personal stories or additional information that will be helpful to the reader. By adding relatable stories to my non-fiction work, my goal is to connect with my reader. When you connect with your reader, you build their trust and gain credibility. Besides, it's always comforting to know that someone else has been down the same road and survived or even came out on top in spite of a difficult experience.

One of the final things I do during the editing process is look for any words that I have used multiple times. Then I get out my thesaurus and look at other words with similar meanings and substitute the ones that make the most sense.

WRITERS INSPIRATION TIP #3: SEEK SUPPORT

Join a writer's group, or work with a mentor or writing coach. While it's great if you have friends or family members who support your writing ambitions, it's even better to have someone in your corner who is familiar with the writing process or the industry because they can support you in ways non-writers cannot understand.

WRITING IS A VERY SOLITARY ACTIVITY.

In most instances writing is a very solitary activity, which makes you vulnerable to attacks of self-doubt. When doubt creeps in, you need someone who can get you back on track. Who better to assist you than someone else who understands because they have faced writer's block, plot pot holes, weak dialogue, boring characters, finding the right company to publish your work, dealing with rejection letters, and a myriad of other writing dilemmas.

The advantages of becoming part of a writer's group are camaraderie, accountability, getting feedback through group-critiquing as you write your story, and gaining valuable information about the writing and publishing industry.

On the other hand, a personal writing coach or mentor guides and encourages you in ways that help you remain focused throughout the writing process. They can help you organize and discuss the stages of your writing project, determine a working schedule, and set a completion date. They help provide an objective perspective on your writing project by identifying what works and what needs work. A good coach can help you develop a clear premise or plot, as well as the right tone, style, and voice so you ultimately produce a coherent and captivating narrative.

I have participated in writing groups and working with a writing mentor. Both were equally beneficial for me. They produced some wonderful friendships, and I received the support, accountability, momentum, guidance and information I needed to navigate my way throughout my journey as a writer.

WRITERS INSPIRATION TIP #4: DON'T GIVE UP YOUR WRITING DREAMS

In high school I had really good writing instructors that helped me cultivate a love of writing. My favorite instructor was Mr. Day, who taught creative writing. Not only was he fun, but he made some of the tedious work we had to do in the module on analyzing works of poetry really interesting.

One of the poems we had to take apart, interpret, and rewrite in our own words was titled, "Jabberwocky." It was written by Lewis Carroll, and is considered one of the greatest nonsense poems written in English. The poem was included in his 1871 novel *Through the Looking-Glass, and What Alice Found There.* The poem is about killing a creature called "the Jabberwock." I still remember the whole class laughing as we worked trying to make up our own nonsense version of the poem.

The problem with high school English classes was that our teachers only focused on correcting our grammar and punctuation. My teachers didn't comment on the quality of the content. Sadly, my work was always returned with a lot of red marks pointing out all my errors. I believed this meant that my writing was sub-par, which shattered my confidence to pursue writing as a career, even though I loved to write. However, I was good at accounting, so I put my focus there. I worked in the accounting field for almost 10 years even though I found it to be monotonous, rigid, and boring. Looking back on it now, I needed those skills to run my own businesses later on in life. So, I really don't regret the years I spent in that field.

In my mid-twenties I decided I wanted to advance in my career, and so I began pursuing a degree in accounting. I was required to take several English composition courses. Because I was older and had more life experience than the other students in my classes, my professor found the essays I wrote to be interesting. As a college student my papers had fewer grammatical errors, and received many positive comments from my professor. She encouraged me to submit something to the college newspaper. I did, and after my article was published I decided I didn't want to spend the rest of my working life in accounting.

I quickly joined a local writers group, and they were supportive. Unfortunately, I heard too many disheartening stories about submission rejection slips from the group members. I knew my newly found confidence could not handle a mountain of rejection at this stage in the game.

My professor had shared with me that my writing was strongest when I wrote about subjects I was familiar with. Around this time, the company I was employed with relocated our office out of state. I became unemployed. I had an 18-month-old daughter and knew all about being a new parent on a tight budget.

So, I started a monthly publication for local parents. It featured places they could take their children to explore in the community at little or no cost. For nine years I published, and wrote *Carroll's Child*. Thankfully, my accounting and business skills helped me succeed. Of course, everything else I needed to know about running a publication I learned from business and marketing books I borrowed from the public library.

> I STILL FELT LIKE A FRAUD AS A "REAL" WRITER.

I will confess that while I did become more confident in my

writing ability, I still felt like a fraud as a "real" writer, because as the editor and publisher I never had to face rejection. However, I was smart enough to pay a retired high school English teacher to proofread the publication each month.

A few years after I began publishing Carroll's Child, the members of my writer's group encouraged me to enter a writing contest in a small publication. I mustered up the courage and submitted a short story. I was so proud when my entry received third place!

Eventually, I became burned out with the hectic pace of running a monthly publication all on my own. A few years later, I was offered the opportunity to write a monthly column for a new local parenting publication. I finally felt like a professional writer because I was paid by someone else for my work.

WRITERS INSPIRATION TIP #5: WRITE TO YOUR STRENGTHS

My work as a non-fiction writer is strongest when I am familiar with or have life experience on a particular topic. I find that drawing from personal experience helps my writing be more evocative, easier for people to relate to, and has a greater impact on the reader.

When I wrote articles and stories about parenting, they were topics I wanted to know about as a parent, as well as the parenting experiences I wanted to share with others. Now that I am into my early fifties, I want to write about Christianity. Of course, the topics will focus on my own struggles as a Christian. For example learning how to having faith in someone I cannot see or touch, understanding the nature of God, why God loves me, how to nurture my relationship with God, how to read and understand the Bible, and how to pray.

I encourage you to take an inventory of the subjects you are passionate about and have meaning to you, and the things in life you have experienced. The next time you sit down to write, look at your list and see how you can incorporate it into your story.

It is my hope that my stories and experiences will inspire your writing. Remember to read a lot, write daily, seek support, refuse to give up on your writing dreams, and write to your strengths. May God bless your creative hearts and minds!

"You don't need endless time and perfect conditions. Do it now. Do it today. Do it for twenty minutes and watch your heart start beating." ~Barbara Sher

ABOUT
KIM MARTIN

Kim Martin has over thirty years of experience in business, writing, and coaching, working in small businesses, corporate and government offices, and educational institutions. For nine years, Kim was the publisher and editor of *Carroll's Child*, a monthly publication for families she founded in 1991. Over the years she has written hundreds of articles on parenting, business, and self improvement.

In 2003, Kim graduated from the "Institute for Professional Empowerment Coaching," and received her certification as a life coach. She started her own coaching practice that same year as a women's empowerment coach. Kim works with women entrepreneurs to foster their personal and professional growth by helping them strengthen their self-confidence, defeat self-sabotage, and overcome self-doubt as they reach their potential and realize their dreams!

Currently, a new chapter is unfolding for Kim that will allow her to focus her considerable experience, skills, and training on helping abused women. She plans on writing books and running a blog about living as a Christian woman in today's challenging and demanding times.

Kim's future creative project is an inspirational blog called *Move Forward in Faith*.

4

BECOME AN AUTHOR WITH ME

ANITA PLAK SEMPRIMOZNIK

This chapter is probably not written in the style some well-established writers with their established voices would probably done it. I've written it in this way on purpose to show you how you can start start small, but still have big dreams and desires you're passionate about. I want to show that you can make baby steps, as I did. Just start and don't get discouraged. Your desire to write a book must be greater than the fears you may be facing right now. And that's ok. Every writer is facing that at some point.

You might be asking yourself, "Who am I to write books? I'm not a writer," or "I've never considered writing a book," or even "I have a deep desire to have my own book, but I don't have copywriting skills."

I hear that a lot. I meet so many people that have a book in them. I see the potential in them and how they could share their knowledge and get paid for it. Unfortunately, *they* don't see that. Yet. Or they may be facing many fears like fear of success, fear of failure, fear of being exposed. And many more.

Could you write a best-selling book? *Of course you could! You just need to be shown how to do it.* Every one of us has a story to tell or knowledge to share.

Honestly, it had never crossed my mind to become a writer. I was convinced I didn't know how to write and that you needed to be a master in writing to write your own book.

Until one day...

SO, HOW IT ALL BEGAN... WHAT INSPIRED ME TO BECOME A WRITER

It was a usual working Wednesday for me. I can't remember exactly what I'd been working on, however, I will never forget how I felt when I received an email from Jay Conrad Levinson, the father of *Guerrilla Marketing*, with the subject line, "Become an author with me."

I couldn't believe my eyes what I had just read. I was staring at my screen, my heartbeat going crazy as I started reading the first lines of the email:

"Here's a guerrilla marketing opportunity that could work really well for you. It's co-authoring a new guerrilla book with me; a book about business or totally unrelated to business," ... and so on.

And somewhere between the lines there was a powerful statement; "As you may already know, a book authored or co-authored by you makes the best business card on the planet. It's a perfect weapon to establish your expertise and credibility."

EVERY ONE OF US HAS A STORY TO TELL.

My hands started shaking, I could hear every sound of the increasing rhythm of my heart beat. Suddenly the whole world around me stopped. Oh my god, I thought. This cannot be true. I was thrilled and a bit shocked at the same time. There were several thoughts crossing my mind. I was really flattered that I had gotten such an invitation from such a great person, and I knew in that instance: *I can do it.* I want to write a book. Of course. How come it didn't occur to me before?

I stopped whatever I was working on prior to reading that email and start writing down ideas for the book I'm supposed to co-author with Jay. I had no doubts, even for a second, that I could do it. No worries, no fears, just pure happiness and an extremely high motivation was driving my inner power that day.

For the next few days I couldn't think about anything else than this email. No matter what I started working on, my mind always got back to thinking about writing the book. The more I thought about co-authoring a book, the more exciting the idea was. I just couldn't stop thinking about it.

On Monday of the following week, I replied with something along the lines of, "Yes, I'd love to join you writing the new book," and asked for more details.

I cannot stress how much adrenalin flowed through my body when I pressed that send button!

A reply to my email arrived soon. As expected, the team at Guerrilla Marketing received hundreds of emails, and they responded with something like "we're putting you on our list to get back in touch with. We will be getting back to interested parties with specifics after we compile our list!"

I was a bit disappointed, but at the same time slightly relieved as my mind started trying to protect me from something new and unknown, from something that I might have been challenged with, and the fears that rose to the surface. I said to myself, *My time will come. I still have plenty to learn.*

A FEW MONTHS PASSED…

I can't say I had slightly forgotten about it, but certainly no longer had any expectations that I could be selected among so many who applied. Until one day that I received another email: "You are one of the people who we are choosing to connect with about coauthoring a Guerrilla Marketing book. You contacted us because you had something to say and we want to help you turn this into reality."

Wow. That almost threw me off my chair! I was so thrilled. I cannot express the feeling of excitement and joy; the feeling that I had gotten a chance to do something great. Something so big I could not perfectly imagine. I was really flattered that I'd gotten such an invitation from such a great person. Who wouldn't want to be part of such a great brand like "Guerrilla Marketing?" Who would be crazy enough to turn down such an offer?

So I followed up until a certain stage. Emails exchanges were going on. I will never forget their words:

Most importantly, congratulations on taking action! So many people want to improve their business or even ask Jay about opportunities to work together but so few actually follow up and take action! Again, Congratulations! Your action is about to really pay off because Jay isn't just looking for co-authors to write books. Jay has already authored and co-authored dozens of books. Rather, he is looking for co-authors with books that can create a new source of revenue for everyone involved through consulting, coaching, events, and information products.

Wow again. No words can express those feelings. I knew I was not the only person who received such an offer. At the end of the day we all know this is business. But for me, this opportunity touched my heart. Deeply.

I personally met Jay Conrad Levinson and his wife, Jeannie Levinson, some time ago when Jay hosted a Guerrilla Marketing conference in our country. Since I was at that time (so I was told) the first certified Guerrilla Marketing coach in my country, I contacted Jay and asked him if we can meet. To my surprise, he replied to me and said yes. I was happy as a small child when given a lollipop!

We spent some great time together with Jay and his lovely wife Jeannie. I never imagined such a great and well-known person would spend time with me and my family. And I guess it was mutual. We treated them like normal people and our friends, not bothering them with some business requests, not asking them for anything. We just enjoyed spending time together. I never even publicly told that story, nor published our photos. I kept this within my family and close to my heart.

I never imagined, or even dared to think I could ever work with Jay. But obviously, he believed in me. He saw something in me, the potential that I couldn't see in myself. And now I know he was right.

Well, you're probably thinking now how lucky I was. But I have to disappoint you. This story doesn't have a happy ending; at least not in the first part. During further email correspondence about the proposed opportunity, when I felt our deal was almost done, I enthusiastically shared my plans with several people. And that was biggest, biggest, biggest mistake I believe I have ever made. None of them truly supported my idea. Quite opposite. They brought to the surface my deepest fears I hadn't even realized I was facing. They planted seeds of doubt in me.

Who am I to co-author book with such a well-known person? I'm not a writer. I've made a great carrier so far, but I'm far away from being such an expert. What if I fail?

And so on. You can imagine. My fears become stronger than my desire, and as I had nobody supporting my dream and passion, I gave up. Yes, I gave up and turned down such a great opportunity. My heart was bleeding when I wrote the last email not accepting the opportunity of a lifetime. But a bit of hope stayed in my heart that there might be another opportunity in the future and by then I might be ready.

Unfortunately, one year later Jay Conrad Levinson passed away. I was sad we lost such a great person. I deeply sympathized with his wife Jeannie. She is so sweet of a person, and they were so nice a couple and so deeply in love. If you didn't know them personally, it would be hard to believe. At the same time it also struck me; it was final. I had missed the greatest opportunity of all time to co-author a book with Jay, and there wouldn't be another chance.

FAST FORWARD FEW YEARS …

Being guerrilla marketer by heart, I continued to follow the work of the Guerrilla Marketing team and continued receiving their newsletters. One day, out of the blue, I received an email from Jeannie Levinson; "We want you to write the next Guerrilla Success book!"

I was shocked. My first thoughts were: *This is it. This is my second chance. There won't be another one. And this time don't blow it! Just go for it!*

Well, you probably figured it out. This time I replied immediately without hesitation. And guess what? I didn't tell a living soul what I was doing. I submitted my idea, passed the selection process and gave my all in following the process with their publisher. After I pressed the send button to submit my manuscript to the publisher, I told my husband and close friends what I had done. And guess what else? They were really surprised.

Check out the book *Guerrilla Success* that I'm referring to on Amazon.com.

Of course, this opportunity was not as shiny as the first one. With this one there were no royalties for me, as we agreed to donate for charity all the royalties from the book sales. And it was ok with me. As for Guerrilla Marketing, Jay and Jeannie were already close to my heart. I wanted to do it. I owed it to Jay because he believed in me. I owed it to myself, as I know what I'm capable of. I just needed to go for it and have the courage to do it. It *was* and *still* is a great feeling, knowing that I'm helping people around the world. I help and inspire readers of my book, as well as those who need help. And, it's helping me in my business. I created a legacy. I have a best-seller and I'm a best-selling author. I was invited to a gala ceremony in Hollywood, where I received a best-seller award from the National Academy of Best-Selling Authors.

> ## START. START SMALL BUT HAVE A BIG DREAM.

"What does your personal story have to do with me," you may be asking. I thought about it for a long time, whether to share this story or not. I don't like sharing my personal stuff. So why would I share something so personal with you, my dear reader?

I'm not trying to sell you a fancy story. I'm sharing this story to help you. To encourage you to start; to start small but still have a big dream and a desire you're passionate about. And to make some baby steps towards it.

Given that you are reading this book, you're:

- Either already established author and just looking for additional inspiration from other authors.
- Thinking of becoming an author.
- You have a book idea, but you're afraid to start.
- Or you received this book as a present; but I'm sure the person gave you this book for a reason. Maybe he or she identified a potential in you.

In any case, I want you to remember how each of us can get an unimaginable opportunity out of the blue, and how fast we can lose it. But there is always another opportunity soon or later if we dare to follow our dreams.

Did I made the biggest mistake I believe I ever made? Or maybe not? Maybe I wouldn't be where I am now. Or maybe I would have had the kind of success I have now years earlier. Or I would be earning so much from royalties that my path would have gone in a completely different direction. Nobody knows; but that's life.

Having said that, I hope my story will inspire and encourage you to listen to your gut feelings and just take action. If you feel this is something you want to do, just do it. Don't wait, and certainly don't listen to people who discourage you from trying. The majority of them aren't able to put themselves in your shoes, and certainly won't give you advice that is in your best interest. They will look at things from *their* perspective and what's working for them, not for you.

> IT ISN'T JUST ABOUT "HOW TO DO" STUFF.

So, work on yourself. Read many books and look at ways to deal with whatever is holding you back or preventing you from being your best. It isn't just about "how to do" stuff; it's much more than that. Therefore, we should never stop learning. Think and act holistically. I know that now. I experienced it. Unfortunately, I learned the hard way.

WRITERS BLOCK AND WHAT INSPIRED ME TO PUSH THROUGH

Before I summarize some lessons from my story that may help you, let me tell you a bit about how I recently experienced so-called "writers block."

I learned the process of writing the book from idea to self-publish to promoting it. I learned how to carve out time and how to get into the creative state of mind when writing. Despite that, I recently experienced a writer's block. It surprised me, as I only had to deliver one chapter. I loved the idea for my chapter topic and had many thoughts on what I would write about. I even thought I had too many ideas for that topic and that I would face a challenge to reduce it to the set length.

So, what's suddenly going on? I'm staring at my screen, looking at my mind-map where I have put down main ideas of what to write about in this chapter, and yet, I feel like my head is empty. Yikes! I cannot understand what is happening. Why is this happening to me? Why now? I have a deadline to meet, and I really want to write this. I'm very knowledgeable and so passionate about passing my knowledge on to other people. I'm even writing books on that topic, and so far so good. It seems there is no logical reason why I'm stuck. Well, this time, whether I like it or not, the whisperer in my mind wins. I close my laptop and decide to postpone it till the next day.

Was this the right decision? I thought so at that moment, but certainly not the next day. The next day, I woke up determined that I would write and finish that chapter in one sitting, no matter what. I knew deep inside there was no reason why I couldn't have done it. So I started setting the stage, preparing myself to step into that creative writing flow that I have experienced every time I'm writing books. I knew that listening to certain talks by mentors or trainers I follow and admire, or reading their blog posts or books related to writing, self-publishing or the topics I'm writing about, would help me get into that state.

So I started to browse for some inspiration, and interestingly I bumped into a blog post of Self-Publishing School. Guess what; it was about writers block. Of course, I immediately read every single word. Funny enough, I already knew all that information.

I read about it though from time to time via blog posts or within books. There is a lot of content available on that topic.

You might be asking what the point is of reading it if you already know all that? I believe it's always worth reading because it's another reminder to help you get back on track, to either become or remain inspired and motivated to proceed. Therefore, I strongly recommend to you, keep learning from different sources, read a lot, and listen to whatever motivates you. Soon or later you'll find what is the driving force you need to get going.

Oh, and I forgot to mention. I completed my chapter the next day. Yeah!

SOME LESSONS AND QUICK WINS I CAN SHARE WITH YOU BASED ON MY STORY

- ✎ Whether you are faced with opportunity or not, listen to your gut feelings. Trust yourself. Just go for it.

- ✎ I started from zero experience in writing. I was so motivated, just did it. First, I wrote everything that came to my mind, everything I wanted to share with my readers. I didn't pay attention to the style or message flow. I just wrote sentences, bullet points, some words, and everything that came to my mind at the time of writing. Then I sorted them in the order I wanted my readers to get the messages I wanted to share. And only then did I fine-tune my sentences and submit my draft to the editor. Now that I know more about writing and self-publishing, I know the first step would be "brain dump" or "mind mapping"; the second part "writing a first draft," and then "self-editing." So, it doesn't matter at what stage of writing you are right now or how you start, just write. You'll learn along the way and get better at it.

- ✎ If you're afraid to start on your own, look for the opportunity to co-author a book, even if it is only for promotional purposes or lead generation. In this way you'll get your "toes in the water" and get a feel for what writing a book means.

- Whether you're trying to work with a publisher or planning to self-publish the book, surround yourself with like-minded people that encourage each other. There are many Facebook and other groups available. Just find the ones that suit you. In a lot of cases there are communities available when you purchase an online course. This may be a good start too.

- Learn about writing and self-publishing. Read books or purchase an online course. When you learn about it, several things become clearer. The whole process becomes simple or simpler as you suddenly know how to do each step. It's easy when you know how.

- Get a coach or mentor. Let them guide you through the process. I cannot stress how valuable that is. Why reinvent the wheel if there is someone who can show you the roadmap to achieve your goals?

- Get yourself an accountability partner for your writing project. Set deadlines and make sure you don't miss them. It works. We often miss the deadline for what we promise to ourselves (there are some exceptions of course), but we rarely miss it when we promise to somebody else.

- Carve out time in your schedule and write regularly. The more you write, the better you'll get at it. Find a way to go into the creative state of mind when writing. For me, it means working in solitude and that I have no distractions around me; no people, no phone, and no internet connection. Just me, my thoughts, and my laptop. Before I start writing I check my "idea cards" for the topic I want to write about. Sometimes I read part of books or watch videos related to my topic to get motivated prior to writing.

- Have a system to write down ideas. It could be mind-mapping, brainstorming sessions, or anything else. I use multiple ways. The ones I just mentioned, and carrying a small note book with me to write down any ideas that occur to me. Some people use their phones to record their ideas. Sometimes I just write a word or a sentence about a certain thing I want to write about later on. At home and in my office I have a box with small note pads. Every time I get an idea, I write it on a card. So when I'm preparing for writing or doing mind-mapping for a new topic, I look at those notes for inspiration.

- ✎ Keep learning to sharpen your skills, to grow as a person and to stay inspired and motivated.

- ✎ Find people that you'll get inspired by. There are some great experts and extraordinary people that I have learned a lot from and who really inspired me along the way.

One was my dear mentor Jay Conrad Levinson, the father of Guerrilla Marketing, whom I had the privilege to personally meet and spend some precious time with. Although he passed away, he left a great legacy that will be with us forever.

Then there is Brendon Burchard, one of the top motivational and marketing trainers in the world, who really inspires me. Every time I listen or watch his trainings, I want more.

Another great example and trainer is Jeff Walker. Every time I listen to his weekly video or any of his trainings, I get inspired and my mind starts producing new ideas.

There are some other authors and trainers I learn from and get inspired by. Just to name a few: Chandler Bolt, Jeff Goins, Nick Stephenson, Joanna Penn, Ray Brehm, Allan Scott, Marisa Peer and many others.

Of course those people I'm mentioning relate to my profession and what I'm passionate about, and are not all necessarily suitable for you. But I'm sure you will find people that you'll get inspired by.

I personally followed all the action steps that I just explained. And now I can do it! I can write and produce good content. I just need to carve out time in my diary and planner and make sure I don't get distracted. Along the way I learned the process. I still read a lot and follow great teachers from different fields of expertise. That's how I grow, learn, and stay on the professional edge; I keep trying something new, following trends, and looking for new ways of doing less for more.

Each of us has certain knowledge to share with other people. Don't waste your talent. Show it to the world. Get the widespread visibility and authority that comes with being a published author.

Create your legacy.

ABOUT

ANITA PLAK SEMPRIMOZNIK

Anita is a Best-Selling Author, entrepreneur and digital marketer with over twenty-six years of senior managerial experience.

Anita's passion is to help people become succesfull with the business of their dreams. She chooses to focus on the positive and focus on clients who appreciate her advice and are ready to do their part in a timely manner. She's brilliant in discovering people's strengths and their opportunities; personal or business.

She is an extremely creative and experienced individual with an extensive business background.

Over half of her career was spent in multinational companies. Her winning combination of Strategic Input, Training, Experience, and Passion is what she offers her clients, associates and partners as the first step towards their business profitability.

Anita is a member of the National Academy of Best-Selling Authors™.

Visit WritingIsArt.com/anitaps to learn more.

5

HOW TO FINISH YOUR BOOK
(WHILE LIVING THE LIFE THAT YOU WANT)

MAYA RUSHING WALKER

THE WRITER'S STRUGGLE AS WE KNOW IT

I wear a bunch of different hats in my day-to-day life, as I'm sure you do. I'm a parent, a spouse, a best friend, a volunteer. I'm also a teacher, a developmental editor, a novelist, and a writer of non-fiction.

We're all living hectic, crazy lives nowadays. But when you have big goals of one sort or another (start a business, get a better job, move to a different state), they have to live alongside other, more mundane things that our various roles in life require. We can't stop making meals, picking up kids from daycare, or showing up on time for work just because we've decided that we want a nicer house, more income, or better opportunities for our children.

And on top of those lofty goals, we still want and need to relax with family and friends, read books, see movies, go on vacation, and otherwise let our brains and bodies rest. In fact, not taking time for ourselves will just lead to burn-out or worse. If we don't rest and recharge, we are even less likely to succeed.

WRITING A BOOK IS A BIG TASK

The dream of writing a book is every bit as big as the dream of a beautiful new house or lucrative new job. Consider this: instead of spending money on a work of art, you're going to make a work of art. It's going to take a long time, and time is money. What's your hourly rate? I'm sure you have one, even if you are retired or at home with kids. How much is an hour of your time worth in the economy? Do the math. You're not buying a Picasso, you're *making* a Picasso (well, a potential Picasso, anyway)! It's a big investment of your time and your life.

> ## WHAT'S YOUR HOURLY RATE?

Writing a book means researching, writing terrible drafts, editing terrible drafts, reading good examples from our chosen genre, and relaxing enough to let our brains do some background processing. You can't just sit down and type until you're finished. That's never how it works.

When we finally allow ourselves to consider it, and we start to think about actually doing it, how do we make this thing happen?

We hear about the writers who burn the midnight oil, wake up at the crack of dawn, or devote their lunch hour to cranking out the great American novel. J.K. Rowling famously wrote *Harry Potter* while at a cafe during her days as a mom on public assistance. There are all sorts of stories about the guts and gumption it takes to write books. Writing is hard work. And *finishing* a book—well, that's even harder than simply *writing* a book.

Successful authors seem to be superhuman. They do it all or they have trust funds and staff or they have dramatic winning-the-lottery-type stories of fame and success, like J.K. Rowling's. But what about us regular people, the ones with kids who get ear infections, neighbors who keep disappearing with our lawn mowers and hedge clippers, and cranky bosses who always seem to notice if we're half a minute over our lunch hour?

MY BATTLE TO WRITE

I'm a homeschooling mom with four kids, a husband who travels all the time, an old ramshackle farmhouse in a rural town, and the usual assortment of time-sucking obligations and last-minute disasters (aging parents, terminally ill pets, cars that break down, insurance claims that don't go through). Every time I sat down to write a sentence, someone interrupted me. It got so bad, I was avoiding phone calls with my mother because I was so anxious about the time I would lose by picking up the phone! I was staying up late, forgetting to eat lunch, and skipping the gym in favor of hunkering down in the car and writing.

The result: a lot of guilt. Because my books still weren't getting written, even with what felt like a lot of sacrifice on my part. Not to mention the fact that I was exhausted and cranky. I wasn't reading books (no time), I wasn't answering email (no time), and I wasn't keeping up with the laundry (no time). Everything around me was a mess.

THE ANSWER

One day, after many years of starting and stopping and starting again, I had an epiphany.

I figured out the answer to the non-stop negative self-talk, the frustration with my lack of progress, and the sense that I wasn't treating myself well. I knew that without rest and an investment in my own mental and physical health, I was grinding myself down. But what about my goal of becoming an author?

Surprisingly, I found that the answer to this was to get rid of my goals. Instead, I asked myself how I wanted to live my life. And the answers were so easy and wonderful, I couldn't believe I had never realized it before.

If you get rid of the big, dramatic goals in your life and replace them with the small, actionable steps that make up the life you feel good about living, you'll end up accomplishing either the big goals that you had wanted in the first place, or other goals you haven't even thought of...or both.

THE PROBLEM WITH GOALS

Goal-setting. I'm not against it. If you want to be a doctor, that's a goal. And if you want to go to Paris on vacation, that's a goal. Writing a book is also a goal. The problem that I have with "deliberately" creating goals is they often come with baggage. Most of us haven't been specifically taught how to make appropriate goals. There is an art to creating goals that make sense; goals are made up of steps, and it's important that the steps are actually doable. What you need to give yourself credit for is not whether you achieve the goal; rather, you need to pat yourself on the back when you execute the steps.

> YOU DON'T ALWAYS HAVE CONTROL OVER THE END GOAL.

Let me say this another way. You have control over the steps. You don't always have control over the end goal. You can't always be sure that you'll attain a big goal. Vacation in Paris? Maybe random obstacles will conspire against you every time you try to get away. All it takes is a sick relative, an airline strike, or a natural disaster to make those plans go bye-bye. But you haven't failed, if you've executed the steps.

You can use those steps to pivot yourself into another goal that you might not have considered, such as a vacation elsewhere or the absolute knowledge that when push came to shove, your ailing relative knew she could count on you for help. The steps that you grit your teeth through and accomplish on the way to the goal—they're honorable and deserve respect.

THE ANTI-GOAL-SETTING PROCESS

So right now you're thinking, "What? How am I supposed to finish writing a book without setting a goal to write a book?"

You're going to do it one step at a time and you're going to do it with an eye on the other things going on in your life.

First, you need a way to keep track of your progress. Use a notebook, a calendar, or your phone. If you like fancy planners and apps that break things down into a bazillion steps, that's fine—but be aware that the act of planning can turn into *over-planning*. Over-planning is a trap. You don't want to make the act of planning "the thing," because finishing your book is actually "the thing!" When goal-planning gets too big and elaborate, the end result will pale in comparison to the complexity and beauty of the plan. You don't want to be underwhelmed with your results, just because your plan was so ambitious.

> YOU NEED A WAY TO KEEP TRACK OF YOUR PROGRESS.

I recommend a daily calendar, and either a notebook or a week- or month-at-a-glance calendar as well. The purpose is to be able to review what you've accomplished. We all understand that we need to make lists in order to prepare to do things, but equally important is a habit of reviewing what you've actually done. The weekly or monthly calendar helps you to do that, or use a notebook to list out what you've done on a daily basis.

Don't obsess over getting these lists perfect. If you use your phone's calendar app or reminder list to remember to do things, you can refer to your phone and list out what you've done in a notebook under a daily or weekly heading.

TIME BLOCK

The second thing you need to do is time block. You're probably already doing this even if you don't realize it. We all block out the things in our lives that aren't movable, even if we don't write them down. So now you're going to log these things. That includes work, family commitments, time on the treadmill, or whatever you need to keep yourself fully functional, healthy, and on top of your responsibilities. Block those out on your calendar or make a list of those things in a notebook. In my case, I'm unavailable on weekdays from about 3:30 p.m. to 9:00 p.m. because my kids have sports practice. I don't bother to pretend that I'll get any personal tasks done during those hours. Instead, I work out, read, or skim online articles and courses.

Realize, right now, that you can't write during those periods. Just forget about it. Release those negative feelings! Instead of fretting about how little time you have, look at that list of activities and realize you are a complex human being with a rich, rewarding life. That's why you want to write a book!

THE STEPS YOU NEED TO TAKE

To write a book, you know you need to do specific things, and there is a natural order in which to do them. For example, eventually you will want to create a writer website, and you will want to do some marketing research. However, it doesn't make a lot of sense to spend tons of time on these tasks *before* you've written your book. So focus on the book. What needs to happen in order for you to get this done?

For non-fiction that might include research, an outline, or brainstorming your topic. For a novel, that might include reading five books in your genre or perhaps reading a few books on story structure. Or you might want to just get started with your writing to see where it takes you. You'll have a general idea of what you need to do, but if you can break those down into smaller steps and record them in your notebook, you can refer to it later. This will help you to remember not to put the cart before the horse; for example, don't try to research self-publishing before you've finished a rough draft.

INTEGRATE YOUR CALENDAR AND THE STEPS

This is where the rubber hits the road. And this is where people often get trapped. The "planning fallacy," first proposed in 1979 by Nobel laureate Daniel Kahneman, suggests that we all underestimate how long a project will take, because we are biased toward optimism and don't take into account actual past experience. I would like to also add that when people are goal-directed, they are thinking about an accumulation of many steps and many factors that they don't actually control. They are trying to place a deadline or strict control on a big undertaking that has lots of moving parts, many of which are dependent on other people, inspiration, or other steps that need to fall into place first.

A good step is something like, "Read for twenty minutes," or "Write for twenty minutes." A step needs to be doable and measurable. It needs to be sufficiently mundane so you know you can do it. It shouldn't stress you out to look at it on your list, nor should it be so vague that you don't know where to start.

Often you will see advice along the lines of, "It'll only take you a month to write a 60,000-word manuscript if you'll just write 2,000 words a day." Look at that sentence for a moment. Let's say that in a four-hour session you can manage 2,000 words. And let's say that you actually can schedule four-hour sessions into your life (I can't, that's for sure). In order to make that "goal" deadline, you can't get sick, you can't take care of a sick kid, you can't have a car break down, you can't have a boss who decides to give you that coveted new project that requires overtime.

If any of those things happen, your goal is toast. And then you're scrambling *just* to make a word-count goal. That's a recipe for self-doubt and failure.

You can stretch that out over a longer period of time, but the same principle applies. Let's say you want to finish your book in a year and you are aiming for a rate of 5,000 words per month. If you're behind at the six-month mark, you're going to be upset with yourself. And that's what I'm telling you does not need to happen.

Don't create a big goal with a definite shape. Instead, create steps with definite shapes, and do it with one eye on your calendar and the other on the rest of your life. For example, as a homeschool parent I am constantly interrupted. So during the day I only attempt steps that will tolerate some interruption. I read, research, or dip into an online course. None of those things need concentration or quiet. Those things are all "steps" on my list of things that have to get done in order to write books.

Raw writing needs quiet, and I don't have huge blocks of time for that, so it has to wait until late at night or first thing in the morning. My steps for the actual writing are things like, "One hour of writing."

RAW WRITING NEEDS QUIET.

Sometimes I don't get the step done. What happens then? It's simple. If I didn't get it done, it means something more important came up (including needing more sleep), and I let it go. I make a note later in my notebook or calendar and I plan another step for another time.

DOCUMENT, DOCUMENT, DOCUMENT

This is important. Make sure to keep an account of what you did and didn't do. And every so often take a quick look. This is why the week-at-a-glance or month-at-a-glance calendar is helpful, although you can do the same thing in a regular notebook. You need to see for yourself what's working and what's not.

When steps are working, keep going. When they keep getting interrupted or aren't producing the results you want too many times in a row, make an adjustment and try again.

THE RESULTS: PROGRESS OR PIVOT

Over time, it should become evident if your steps are leading to the kind of productivity that will produce a book. What should also become clear are the ways in which you are interrupted, stalled, or unable to get to the step. Identify whether it's the step, the environment, or your resolve that's the problem. All of these issues are fixable, but they need different kinds of adjustments. If you still want to write that book, you'll find a way to correct the problem. You may also discover that you don't want to write the book after all or maybe it's not about writing a book, it's about writing *this* book.

Allow yourself some room to pivot. Remember, you're not trying to write a book *at all costs*. You're trying to create a piece of art while you're doing other important things in your life. You're allowed to make changes to the project as you go along. You're also allowed to make changes to the individual steps.

A VIRTUOUS CYCLE

The eventual result, I hope, should be a virtuous cycle of positive movement, reasonable adjustment, and a comfortable fit for the varying roles and responsibilities that all of us have in our lives. No more, "I'm such a loser, I can't stick to a schedule." No more, "I'm such a loser, I yelled at my significant other because she interrupted my writing time."

Pivot if you need to. Adjust if you need to. It's not unreasonable to decide that for the time being, your sick cat takes priority. Or that you want to take an online course, so your 10 a.m. block of writing time is going to be devoted to that instead. When you look at your calendar or your notes, you'll know this was a choice, which is why you wrote less in August than June.

MY OWN VIRTUOUS CYCLE

As I mentioned earlier, I'm the homeschooling mom of four. I struggled for a long time, trying to fit everything into my crazy life and blaming myself for being disorganized and unfocused. My floors were dirty, and I was having a hard time keeping up with friends, yet I couldn't seem to finish a book project, even after years of writing and completing first drafts that were really pretty good.

I thought that maybe it would help to take a class, so I did that. Nope, that didn't help. It just bogged me down with more guilt because I couldn't keep up with the pace of the assignments. Then I joined a mastermind group that I paid for, and while I made friends and learned some new approaches to book marketing, it didn't lead to any new insights about finishing projects. I joined a writing group, listened to podcasts, and signed up for more courses. Nope. Nope. Nope.

One day I looked around at the dirty floors and the heap of unfolded laundry and thought about the things that were working and the things that were not. And I realized something. I don't really care about the floors or the laundry, because those are things that I "rinse and repeat" all the time. There's no forward motion with housework; I don't get better, it doesn't get easier or more interesting. And frankly, no one in my house cares if I fold clean laundry or not. It's clean, isn't it? But the things that I truly care about show the evidence of my care, and these are long-term things. My kids are healthy, happy, and getting a spectacular education (if I say so myself). My older two kids were extremely successful in college. My younger two continue to push forward in their schoolwork and do amazingly well. All of them turned into top athletes in their sports. They are caring people who pursue their own passions with vigor. I can say without exaggeration that I played a role in this, because I drove them to practice every day, fed them the calories they needed, and made room for their passions in our household and in their lives.

Those things don't happen overnight. A family is a long-term project with steps that you execute day after day, week after week. You focus on the single step in front of you (getting to practice, making the healthy meal, nagging them to get to bed early) and you see it as an investment. Sometimes it doesn't go well and you have to stop and figure out what isn't working.

My son was having a difficult time balancing two sports, volunteering, and carrying a huge load of schoolwork in high school. When he came to us for help, we had to make some big household changes so he could get what he needed. That was a pivot, and it was worthwhile because we were focused on taking the steps that would support his growth.

I took a long look at my literary work, and when I told my critical inner voice to leave me alone for a moment I saw a lot of positive forward motion in what I'd done. My writing course taught me a new way to look at my writing. My mastermind group showed me that I don't have to buy into generic internet marketing advice, and I made writing friends from that group who are still friends today.

My problem was not *what* I'd done. It was the *way* I was looking at it. I was evaluating my work from the top-down goal viewpoint, because no, I hadn't yet completed my projects. But I completed lots of steps, and together those steps actually make sense. They just make sense differently from the one big goal I set for myself, which is to get my work out into the world.

AND...THE BOOK GOT DONE!

After I realized that I wasn't actually lame and unproductive, things changed. I could see that I was on a different timeline from someone who kicks out a book a month and perhaps doesn't have a family to take care of or other projects in life that need and deserve time and attention. For example, I let my kids interrupt me at will. That's a choice I make. I make that choice because I can see the evidence that it works. I've launched two young people into the world and I'm ready to launch two more. Those are my priorities right now. And yes, it slows me down. But meanwhile, I am putting the work into my own dreams step by step.

Chapter by chapter, I got feedback and criticism from beta readers on one of my completed works that helped me to edit my draft. I sent it out to a copyeditor, and when I got it back, I dug in again.

I did the work step by step, chapter by chapter. I no longer berated myself for not working quickly enough and not having the four-hour chunks of time I wish I had. I wrote down in my notebook, "one hour of editing" many times.

And the book got done. And the best part of this is not even the book! It's what I learned from continuing to work on it. Let's say the book hadn't gotten done. Now that I don't obsess on the goal, I just accept that maybe I don't really know what the goal is yet. I think it's to finish a book, but it could be something else. All the pieces that went into finishing my first book can legitimately be applied to something else, after all.

If you really want to write a book, don't draw up a mondo plan and then go gangbusters on it. I urge you to consider the small steps that go into book writing and see where to put those in your daily life. Don't discount those small steps, because you don't know where they'll lead. They may lead to something bigger and better. If you keep on going, those steps are what you'll need. This is how a family is created or a career is constructed or a book is completed.

You can do this. One step at a time. Stop the self-judgment. Keep making neutral observations on the page, on your calendar, in your notebook. And every week or so, take stock. What have you done? Why and why not? The things that are important to you should be right there, right in front of you. If you like it, great. If not, pivot. And your book will get done—if it's meant to be—one step at a time, without making you crazy and without taking over your life.

> STOP THE SELF-JUDGEMENT

ABOUT
MAYA RUSHING WALKER

Maya Rushing Walker writes novels from her 1780s farmhouse in northern New England. She is a graduate of Georgetown's School of Foreign Service and has a master's in East Asian Studies from Harvard. Multicultural settings and historical fiction are her thing, as well as romantic novels set in old and New England, written under her pen name, Cassandra Austen (yes, Jane's sister!).

She speaks Japanese (well) and Arabic (badly), and while she is originally from Honolulu, she has also lived in Saudi Arabia, Tunisia, Egypt, and Jerusalem. She is the nerdy, hip mom of four great homeschooled kids who refuse to let her grow old. Find her multicultural fiction at MayaRushingWalker.com and her sweet romance novels at CassandraAusten.com.

THE WRITER AS ALCHEMIST

DREW BECKER

Years ago at Denver's Poet Day in downtown Denver, Colorado, I was interviewed by a reporter who asked me why I wrote. The response came from my core; I had no time to think and heard myself answer without crafting my reply.

I was surprised to hear myself as I explained: "The experience begins as a twinge in the middle of my chest. I can ignore it for a few days, but it persists no matter what I do. I can try to shake it off. The feeling will retreat for hours or a day, but then it's back. It's as though I am weighted down with the idea until I release it from my mind and transfer it to paper or screen. In this sense writing is a burden."

I also find if I do not write for a week or so I feel congested; not physically, but rather in an emotional or spiritual sense. Once an idea begins to germinate, it will not leave me alone. What might begin as a fleeting thought grows into a project begging to be done. When I work on longer pieces, the effort demands my attention. This obsession is likely to poke me as I am working on other projects and during sleep. I am not complaining; however, sometimes I think I'd rather be left alone. That feeling does not last long. Writing is a compulsion for me as it is for many other authors.

WRITING IS CONNECTED TO THE BREATH OF LIFE.

A few months later a colleague asked me how I write. I could not answer her at the time, and was at a loss for years. The question plagued me and reoccurred until I stumbled upon the correct response. I had to dedicate some time and meditation to find the answer for myself. What I discovered was a simile: Writing is like inhaling and exhaling; it is connected to the breath of life. I wondered what is the in-breath process and the out-breath practice and what activities are related to each?

Inhaling comprises collecting and assembling ingredients, drawing them to my consciousness, swirling them around, and concocting a creative cloud. The pieces that comprise this ether might originate as snippets of conversation, gestures I observe, research about a related topic, a story I hear, or thoughts that come in meditation or while falling to sleep. I often make notes to remember these tidbits. Later I return to those notes and see how they relate to one another. My next step is building an outline or sequence. Like fitting puzzle pieces together, I arrange and rearrange these sometimes disparate pieces until I form a rough version I like.

This amorphous haze is then left to congeal. Although writing mentors taught me to put a manuscript away and look at it later, I didn't realize that this tactic is also useful during the composing process. I focus a personal lens on the mixture and review it for potential. It is then time to put my spin on it and fashion a draft of the result. What I have concocted is then ready for the out-breath stage.

The exhale is more elusive. I stick my metaphorical fingers in the brew and massage it. This sends me into flights of fancy and frees my mind from preconceptions about what I thought I would write at the beginning of the process. I open to the discovery of something I had not imagined previously. As the words roll out, I play with them and allow them to make new connections and permutations. I open to unseen forces, maybe cosmic, maybe angelic, maybe divine, perhaps from a special guide or the muse. I envision my desired reader and share the "results" as the words flow onto the page or screen. Once made concrete, I expel it to make room for the something new.

On occasion the original idea and organization is better than any of my revisions, but I rarely use what first comes to me word for word. The exception is with some poetry that springs fully developed from my mind.

Stumbling upon my creative process emerged when I was not directly thinking about it. One of my poems, "Alchemist," revealed my creative process to me, but it was later before I understood that I had discovered it. The poem combines the mechanistic (inhaling) and magical (exhaling) processes in the creation transformation.

ALCHEMIST

average analogs
banal bridges
common combs
dinosaur decanters
transmutations
phantasmagoria
quickness of wrist
the mist the mind
mesmerized inside

> *the mime*
> *the muse*
> *slipping through*
> *to choose the passage*
> *dance begun*
> *film unfolding*
> *phoenix guiding*
> *grinding mechanisms*
> *the brain stumbles*
> *surrender to magic*
> © drewbecker 1976

The transformation of thought into a written form has two parts: mechanistic and magical. First comes the mechanistic followed by the magical.

MECHANISTIC

The mechanistic phases of writing correspond to the in-breath. Since I have been writing for decades, many of these mechanical processes are done subconsciously. Some of these actions are part of the writing process, while others are employed during editing. Many of these techniques are blended as I work through a blog, article, book, or story. To show the process, I will delineate each of the parts, although the mechanical techniques congeal in the magical phase.

- I begin with content and context. I decide on my subject matter or message and consider audience and purpose.
- I build an outline or a mind map to have a blueprint.
- I embellish by using poetic language to paint pictures and anchor the ideas in ways the audience can relate to them. Using similes and metaphors, making analogies to common tasks, and employing other devices like alliteration,

assonance, and rhyme make this possible.

- With my direction in mind, syntax comes next. I build my prose sentences or poetic lines and make word choices to shape the writing.

- I consider semantics: What do the words mean to me, to others around me, to the culture as described in dictionary definitions?

- And most importantly, I add stories where applicable, since that's what I like to read.

Let me do a post-mortem on a blog post I wrote recently. When I write a blog for a client who is a CPA and a Certified Financial Planner, I need to stretch to write something new every week. Most of his clients are self-employed, as am I, but may have had jobs in companies in the past.

The inhale stage includes perception and interpretation. Movement through these two parts advances the writing.

Perception is the first part, where I seek a fresh approach to my topic. Interpretation follows, where I consider my experience of a situation and hunt for a collective facet my readers will appreciate. One of the themes I chose was whether his clients and prospects were getting large enough refunds. I began with my experience with refunds when I worked in a corporate job. I was excited to get my refund and fantasized about how I would spend it. More recently, I have owned my own company and most years have to pay taxes and do not get that windfall. It was easy to tap into my current emotional reaction to this: dreading doing taxes and scrambling to find money to pay the tax bill. The Beatles' song "Taxman" danced in my head.

I imagined many of his self-employed readers having similar reactions. What could I write to entice them to contact this CPA? I wanted to use a poetic device to capture their emotions, and a metaphor was a perfect technique. As you may know, a metaphor is created by attributing one idea to an unrelated one. Fishing came to mind. I explored what words I could use to connect these two concepts. I reviewed my words in hopes that they would arouse in others what they evoked in me as I wrote. In this case, I made the reader the main character in the story and addressed him or her directly.

MAGICAL

The magical phase of writing corresponds to the out-breath. While considering how I would present the topic, my mind reflected on my experience working for myself. Instead of waiting for the refund check, I now scurry to scrape together money for my tax bill. I remembered fishing with my dad before I was in my teens. I usually ended up with nothing at the end of the day after hours of sitting still with difficulty. What I caught was too small, and I was instructed to throw it back into the stream. I was fine with that because they weren't big enough to cook and eat. I took this flight back into my childhood and forgot about the drudgery of taxes for the moment.

> THE BLOG POST ALMOST WROTE ITSELF.

The disappointment of hooking a little fish and throwing it back connected those childhood fishing experiences with filing my taxes. If I would have tried to discover how I made this connection, I couldn't come up with an answer. I only understood that I could play with words about fishing to explain the emotion behind a small refund, no refund at all, or having to pay taxes with my return. The blog post almost wrote itself once all these magical connections were made. Here is the substance of the post:

SMALL FRY REFUNDS

As tax refunds are being sent, which will you be:

- Delighted with your big catch?
- Disappointed with your puny refund and ready to throw it back?
- Depressed that the shark caught you?

Don't settle for an empty fishing trip and the post-April 15th blues.

Be sure you are getting the best possible return with all allowable deductions. When you work with a CPA and a Certified Financial Planner, your financial plan can save money on taxes.

If you were disappointed or depressed by this year's tax bill or small refund, now is the time to make a change for next year. Our CPAs can begin working with your financial situation and get you set for taxes next year. Don't settle for small fry returns; reel in the big one.

Call today to set an appointment and prepare for a successful catch next tax season.

The way I write—and I suspect a number of other writers do as well—is by combining the mechanisms and magic of writing. We endeavor to transform our dreamscapes and ideas, characters, plot, and stories to demonstrate concepts, instructions about how to achieve results, and other elements, putting them onto paper.

I used the previous example of the blog post because it is small enough to dissect and examine the process. When working with a nonfiction essay or book, the process is the same but more detailed, and the sequence is repeated numerous times for each subchapter, chapter, section, and finally for the manuscript as a whole.

The mechanical or in-breath activities include creating the structure—whether employing an outline, a mind map, or other device. Then each part of the structure can be isolated to build the necessary elements. I pull from different sources: Here is my idea about the topic; there is a story to illustrate; there is the research to back it up; there is a personal interview to add more value. I gather and do a preliminary assembly of these and other pieces. All of this is still in the notes stage.

As in the example of the blog, the next step is more difficult to define. After leaving the notes for a little while, I return to them and make some novel semblance of the part of the manuscript I am working on. Most of this is intuitive, since the outside structure is already built, but not cast in stone. I let my mind play with the pieces and assemble and reassemble them. Sometimes this is a lengthy process; on other occasions it happens quickly. The results are a rough draft.

I put the writing away for a few days after completion, and I am often surprised at the results. As I reread it, I subconsciously go through the same processes and spend time editing. I usually comb through the manuscript or article at least three times.

Once I think it is good enough, I turn it over to an editor. For a longer work, I might send it out to beta readers to get their input before submitting to my editor. Working with beta readers is a recent addition to my process, but one I recommend if you can find generous people to comment on your work.

The first time I tried, I sent out a series of questions. I learned quickly to just ask for comments. Some readers will send general remarks; others will reply with detailed suggestions, and others may actually edit your work.

With the beta readers' comments, I integrate the suggestions I think will improve my draft. I set the manuscript aside, then return later to edit it again. Once I have a final draft, I send it to my editor for a final proofing.

No matter what the length or genre of my writing, I employ part or all of this process. It requires both structured and imaginative phases. This necessity of performing both activities is one of the greatest challenges for writers. Some have told me they love crafting the sentences and paragraphs word-by-word. Others have confided they prefer the creative, free-flowing phase. Most writers will agree that they engage in both to achieve a remarkable manuscript.

When I write poetry, the combination works a bit differently. I rarely structure a poem before writing, but rely on the magic of inspiration to get the writing started. I usually write out as much as will lend itself to my conscious mind and then put the piece aside. I return to the draft of the poem to agonize over each word, refine the rhythm, improve the flow. If the poem has rhyme, I make sure they work well and do not disturb the rhythm. The next step is to read the poem aloud and listen for flaws. Finally, I fix any passages, lines, or words that are not exactly what I am wishing to portray, and repeat until I am satisfied the poem conveys what I intended.

Writing fiction is similar, but with important differences. I need to have a clear idea of the plot laid out as an outline or chapter summaries. I try to write all the way through based on the outline or chapter synopsis. However, many times as my characters communicate with me (yes, I do have dialogues with them), they will alter the plot in ways I had not imagined. This is one way the magical phase emerges. I also will write basic descriptions of locations and what characters look like and return later to flesh them out.

After writing a draft, I edit. I make sure that all the characters maintain their personalities even if they do something that may seem unusual. I tighten the plotline where I can and review the descriptive passages to assure myself they convey the mood and visuals I want my readers to see.

Finally, I re-read from beginning to end. This can be difficult after working with the manuscript for long periods. However, I will often find last-minute improvements. Then comes the time to ready the final draft for formatting and perhaps a final view by an editor.

I suspect all writers are alchemists, spinning value and entertainment out of that illusive ether. We all take the straw of everyday life and spin it into the gold that readers relish. The finished product may be remarkable to the reader, but it is nothing short of miraculous to the writer.

ABOUT
DREW BECKER

Drew Becker has writing in his blood. He began writing before the age of 10, but didn't publish until 1976. He abandoned teaching English after a decade and took time for odd jobs: working in restaurants, bartending, and cab driving to pay the rent as he dedicated himself to writing.

His work in corporate was primarily as a technical writer. As an entrepreneur he teaches business writing and creates social media for clients. His most recent passion is to help independent authors publish.

In his latest book, *The Joyful Brand: Personal Branding for Authors, Speakers and the Rest of Us*, Drew reveals how to create a powerful personal brand. This type of branding occurs from the inside out and begins with your purpose and passion, allowing you to be distinct, notable and authentic.

He has been published in *The Original Relocation Guide, Business Leader, The Denver Post, The Rocky Mountain News* and other periodicals.

His publishing company, *Realization Press*, has released over 20 books both fiction and non-fiction.

As a coach he works with first-time and published authors and business people to help with writing, branding and marketing.

Visit RealizationPress.com to learn more.

7

A WRITER'S GOTTA WRITE

JAMIE WHITE WYATT

You don't have to publish a best-selling book to qualify as a writer. If you write, you are already a writer! Own it!

From the time I could grasp a crayon, I "wrote" squiggles. I always loved to write. By second grade, I was creating illustrated stories in notebooks. ("The Big Splash" documented my accidental fall from a powerboat around age 7!)

I was on my high school newspaper staff, and co-edited the year book. I worked for my university's student newspaper and majored in journalism. Non-fiction writing has always been my happy place.

Over 30 years ago, I started writing a book about family traditions. Then "life" happened. Serious health issues. Career changes. A move. Kids. Parents' terminal illnesses. You get the picture.

I put my book project away... still, I wrote! I wrote stories about memories and family history and filed them on my computer. I wrote articles for newspapers and newsletters. I composed ads and press releases for my advertising agency, and wedding articles and gown descriptions for my bridal shop. I became the go-to writer/editor for various non-profits and for organizations where I volunteered.

About ten years ago, I saw a "Story Call Out" for Chicken Soup for the Soul. My creative juices went into overdrive! I had never considered submitting stories for book projects. I edited and submitted two stories about family traditions. I did not tell a soul.

Both stories were accepted and published! I submitted more stories. They were also published. That victory was my impetus to soldier on. I was officially a "published author" and began calling myself a writer.

> # WRITING CAN FULFILL YOUR PERSONAL GOALS.

If you don't have a definitive plan for your writing, you might try looking for new ways to utilize your skills and experience. Whether or not you are traditionally published, you can find satisfaction through writing that is meaningful or fulfills your personal goals. Examples of personal goals are: preserving family history, positioning yourself as an expert, sharing personal and professional knowledge, or earning money—either by selling your writing or contracting to write for others.

I heard Kristen Joy speak at a conference, met her, and tried several of her courses. In her *Kindle in 30-Days Challenge* I was inspired to complete a rough draft for my 30-year-old family traditions book. That book turned into a series which is close to being finished! After another of Kristen's courses, I published a full-color memoir cookbook with photos and handwritten recipes from a deceased childhood friend.

Kristen also teaches ways to repurpose and repackage writing projects. Many years ago, I self-published two cookbooks to give friends instead of Christmas cards. The first was favorite recipes from all categories. The second was cookie recipes. Both were compiled from family and friends. I plan to repurpose those cookbooks as Kindle books and subscription or book bonuses.

I also began speaking. I love writing speeches with accompanying handouts for my audiences. Those speeches and handouts are being used as the basis for future book projects.

In examining my motivations for writing, I found that my inspiration generally fits into these categories:

7 MOTIVATIONAL P'S

1. Passion
2. Preparation
3. Pain
4. People
5. Projects
6. Pressure
7. Payment

Passion: For an issue or subject. Examples: faith, family, drug abuse, combatting sex trafficking, and so forth.

Preparation: Entices us to write. It is easier to be creative and productive in comfortable, quiet, well-stocked spaces, where we have everything we need, including drinks, snacks and supplies, readily available.

Pain: Over a situation, event, or death. Examples: memorials or eulogies, tragic events, and such.

People: This category is wide open. Examples: writing to inspire an individual or group, writing about an inspirational person or group, writing about family, friends, heroes or villains, and more.

Projects: This can include articles and blog posts, but usually involves more detailed writing, like books or a series of them.

Pressure: Usually imposed by the timeliness of the subject, or external deadlines.

Payment: Includes actual monetary compensation, but might also be exposure through publicity, promotion, or opportunities to speak and sell books, all of which motivate me!

Writing, proofreading, and publishing are much less costly and intimidating than they used to be. Many programs and apps help streamline the processes. Even though processes are technologically easier, I still wrestle with these roadblocks and distractions—real or imagined. You may, too! Beware of these common roadblocks:

7 DISTRACTING P'S

1. Procrastination
2. Prioritization
3. Phones
4. Pride
5. Proficiency
6. Proofreading
7. Publishing

Procrastination: Putting off writing by allowing distractions and excuses to sidetrack and delay us.

Prioritization: Having too many projects going.

Phones: We all tend to waste time on our phones, when we could be writing!

Pride: Worrying about what others will think about our writing; questioning our talent.

Proficiency: Worrying if our writing is grammatically and structurally correct, and measures up to the technical standards for well-written projects.

Proofreading: Trying to make things perfect; hesitating to let a proofreader do their job because our writing "needs more work."

Publishing: Allowing ourselves to be overwhelmed with all the details and "moving parts" of both the digital and print publishing processes.

Being aware of and intentional with the Motivational and Distracting "P's" will help you stay focused and be more productive in writing!

After aligning your motivational P's and overcoming the distracting ones, you'll be well on your way to the finished product: your book! However, one very important "P" remains: Preparation—for Success!

We usually think of achieving success as arriving at the "Happy Ending;" fame, fortune, and bliss. That isn't always the case. I have two friends whose lives were absolutely torn apart in the aftermath of publishing their books. What was anticipated as a happy event, quickly deteriorated. Both women were blindsided by the affect fame had on their marriages.

Both friends launched and promoted their books to Amazon Bestseller status and regional fame. One published a second book. Husbands and children were jealous of the amount of time book promotions and events required. They also did not like the attention being focused on them because of their wives' and mothers' sudden celebrity.

Both women were strong professionals, who had successfully juggled family and careers for years. Both husbands were initially supportive of their wives' writing. Both women were already locally well-known. Their successes were celebrated in their communities. Both authors did speaking and book signings for local and regional events.

It was a total shock to my friends that their husbands did not enthusiastically support their successes. It severely dampened—and actually ruined—what should have been peak experiences for my friends.

The men had not expected their wives' newfound celebrity nor the time commitment required for book promotion. Neither man liked the disruptions caused by their wives' new ventures and were woefully unprepared for the attention focused on their families because of it.

One friend let success go to her head; the other remained very grounded. One lady got swept up into destructive behavior, while the other one's husband self-destructed over his wife's book. Both couples began the divorce process. Last I heard, my younger friend is trying to re-establish her family. The repercussions in the other family, even after a 40-year marriage, were too devastating to repair. For now, both women are abandoning their dreams of writing.

This happens to be a story about women authors. Men are not immune. I know of men who have been similarly affected when their wives could not adapt to the changes brought about by their successes.

The possibility of success and celebrity should be considered. Please do some soul searching and have candid discussions with your family about the perils of instant celebrity. Set boundaries on your time. Guard your hearts. Guard your family's privacy. Limit publicity if necessary.

Also consider how you and your family might handle the *opposite* of success. What if your book is not as successful as you hope? How will you deal with disappointment and possible financial loss?

Try not to go into book publishing with pre-conceived and potentially unrealistic goals. You may not make much money. You may not get interviews. You may get poor reviews.

You may need to be content with the fact that you completed your task, or be satisfied with putting your message out and trusting that those who need it will find it. You may never know whose lives you touched, or even whose lives you may have saved.

Unmet expectations might tempt you to quit writing. Don't. If you have a story write it, even if it is just for you, for now. A writer's gotta write! Writing and finishing your book—or even a project—makes you a success! Your message is in your heart and you write for a reason.

Don't ever lose focus on the fact that your family is more important than 15 minutes of fame and Amazon best-seller status. It is not "failure" to defer your dreams until the timing is better. You need to be well-grounded and prepared for success. Your family also needs to understand all the possibilities and be on board.

Fame, jealousy, popularity, money, disappointment, busyness, and failure are all potential pit-falls for authors. Please make sure you and your family are prepared for how these "roadblocks" might affect you all.

On the bright side, there are still "happy endings!" I currently have three author friends whose writings have evolved into tv and movie projects, and some very lucrative national and international speaking engagements. These friends are intentional about budgeting their time and have the full support of their families!

> # CONSIDER HOW YOU'LL HANDLE SUCCESS... AND ITS OPPOSITE.

I also have friends whose writing successes fall somewhere between these two extremes. Knowledge is power. Forewarned is forearmed.

I look forward to hearing about your experiences and victories!

ABOUT
JAMIE WHITE WYATT

Jamie White Wyatt is a writer, speaker, and Bible teacher. She loves sharing her joy through speaking about faith, family, and prayer. Jamie has stories in multiple *Chicken Soup for the Soul* books. She is currently writing a book series on family traditions and Christian living. Since starting an advertising agency at the age of 21, Jamie has owned several successful businesses, including a bridal and formal shop, a gourmet food business, and a petroleum marketing company.

Jamie would love to hear from you! traditionplace@gmail.com

MY RULES OF WRITING

HOW I STAY INSPIRED AND ON TRACK

KD PRYOR

I am a writer and a bit of a rule follower. Well, I follow rules that make sense and keep my life in order. Okay I follow rules most of the time—I wish I were a rebel, but I'm really not. I find that the best rules to follow are the ones I make up. And to that end, I have a few rules of writing that keep me motivated, on track, and productive.

I have seven rules or concepts to share with you. I wanted to come up with a neat acronym so they'd be easy to remember. I did not. DRICBRE doesn't mean a thing. But it gives a structure, and for a rule-oriented person like me that's a good place to start anything. Let's get started.

To be a productive writer, one must write. I've struggled with this concept because, unbeknownst to non-writer types, writing is hard work. But two words help me to start and continue on my writing path: dedication and discipline.

THE DOUBLE D'S: DEDICATION AND DISCIPLINE.

Dedication, for me, is the heart-felt commitment to your writing; an inner conviction that writing is your life purpose and you have to write.

When you next sit down to write, take a moment in stillness and imagine your life without writing as a part of it. What would you lose if you stopped writing, choosing to let this path go? What will you gain if you choose to follow through and write? Your dedication flows from the inner responses to these questions. If you've realized you gain more by staying with writing, or you lose too much if you let your passion go, you have discovered you are dedicated. But how dedicated are you? It may help to rate your level of dedication from a one (low) to a ten (high). If you are deeply dedicated, it is easier to find your discipline.

> DISCIPLINE IS A CONTRACT WITH YOURSELF.

Discipline is the internal vow to stay true to the structure you've created in order to complete your work. Discipline is a contract with yourself. When you are disciplined, you are saying that writing is important and you will devote yourself to your writing goals. In order to stay disciplined, you must have a structure to follow. Developing this structure is the next writing rule or concept I will discuss.

CREATING A WRITING ROUTINE: RITUALS YOU FOLLOW IN YOUR WRITING LIFE

Knowing you are dedicated to your writing is an important first step. But it is too easy to bask in the knowing and fail to get the work done. That's why you have to formulate a writing routine. Your routine is a series of rituals you follow each time your write. As you become accustomed to your routine, you will begin to program your subconscious mind to recognize this process. Follow the steps you create faithfully and they will become second nature.

The first step in your routine is to determine when, how often, and for how long you will write. Each of us is different with unique demands upon our time. Blog posts and writing books offer all sorts of ideas about why we ought to write in the morning or at night or standing on our heads. But only we writers can decide this for ourselves. If you can write three days a week from noon to two, perfect. If your schedule is different each day, figure out when you can fit writing into your life. Whatever you decide, make it official by marking your calendar and creating a writing date with yourself. Other details you need to decide on include how many words or pages you want to accomplish in a given time, where you want to write, and any other nonnegotiable details to make your session fruitful.

I will confess that I write at different times each day. I would love to get up very early and get started, but I haven't found success with this process. Instead, I prefer to exercise early in the morning. Exercise sharpens my mind and puts me in a good mood. When I come to my desk in the late morning or early afternoon, I'm ready to get going. I like to start my writing session with a short meditation to still my mind and focus on my next task; eloquently placing words upon a page or computer screen. Whether or not I actually accomplish eloquence is up for debate, but I have a few other rituals that matter to me.

I have a dedicated office space where I write and a large desk where I can spread things out. I like to keep my thesaurus next to me for quick reference. And I prefer my real thesaurus to the computer-generated ones, although I use both when needed. I always have a notebook for ideas and water on hand. Finally, I get up every thirty to forty minutes and move to avoid backaches later.

There are myriad ideas to include in writing rituals. Some other important ones to consider include turning off all devices—like phones—in order to limit distractions, and setting a timer if you are on a strict schedule.

Once you have a routine in place, it's important to have something to write about. That's where the third writing concept comes into play.

THE DOUBLE I'S OF INSPIRATION AND IDEAS.

Writers need inspiration to fuel their craft. Inspiration leads to more definite ideas about what to write. Whether you are writing fiction or non-fiction, memoir or poetry, you can't finish a project without a thought about where to start, how to proceed, and what constitutes 'The End'. I've written both non-fiction and fiction and have found that my inspiration for each comes from different sources.

My non-fiction book, co-authored with a colleague, stemmed from a practice we studied and became certified to coach. Because the process is excellent for relieving stress, and because I had two kids in college when we decided to write the book, we chose to focus on stress relief for college students. This inspiration leading to the idea for a book for college students came from a professional background and is very different from the inspiration which informs the fiction I write.

I'm a visual person and love houses—all types of

> # WRITERS NEED INSPIRATION TO FUEL THEIR CRAFT.

houses—from small quaint cottages to large rambling estates. Architectural features, like windows and doors, can be very evocative. The lit windows of early evening or a pair of bright, red shutters make me wonder about the space beyond the opening. Doorways, like windows, also spark questions about who lives or works behind the entrance, whether the doors are shabby and weather-beaten or ornate and colorful. When I notice a window or doorway I find particularly intriguing, I start to wonder what it might be like to live in the house or building attached. Is there a family inside getting ready for dinner? Are children doing homework? Or is what I see a front for unhappiness, anger, or pain? A story begins to form.

The first novel I wrote was inspired by a house situated next to an old graveyard. I'd been by the house before, but on this particular late afternoon I was approaching it from a new direction. Something in the angle, the shifting daylight, the slope of the stones, combined to make me wonder what, if anything, might occur between the basement of the house and the graves tilting in the cemetery. I was certain something intriguing could be going on, and as soon as I was home I started to brainstorm ideas for the Young Adult paranormal novel which became *The Portal's Choice*.

What are other ways to find inspiration that leads to ideas for wonderful books? I find that walking is a great source of inspiration. Nature is full of great ideas, as long as we are always aware and noticing. Those are two words I like to remember wherever I am and whatever I'm doing. I also find that being quiet, listening, and considering the people and objects in my surroundings provide new ideas for stories.

As you begin to bring your inspired ideas to life on the page, it's time to call up the fourth writing concept, another double letter beauty.

THE DOUBLE C'S OF COURAGE AND CONFIDENCE.

Sitting down to write is intimidating. Even more, it can be scary. What if the words don't flow? What if no one likes what you write? This is when you have to draw on your inner courage and forge ahead. Use your dedication and discipline to summon up confidence as you sit down, even on the days you don't want to.

> ## YOUR FIRST EFFORT WON'T BE YOUR LAST.

Having your writing routine in place helps you to stick to your commitment and get the work done. Put the words on paper or on the screen. Your first effort won't be your last. Your work will be edited before you reader gets their hands on it, but you won't succeed if that first draft never gets done.

Ways to increase your courage and bolster your confidence include working with a writing buddy, scheduling writing dates, or even taking a writing class. I'm part of a writing workshopping class. In class I meet and interact with other writers, read and constructively critique their work, and receive feedback from them on my work in progress. Having to turn in writing keeps me motivated, and interacting with others who love to write as I do is inspiring.

On those days when no amount of dedication, discipline, routine, ritual, courage or confidence can help you find the words you're searching for, you need writing concept five.

A BREAKTHROUGH

A writing breakthrough is a coming back to your core writing self. All writers lose their way. We all get stuck. Most of us have even stopped writing when the going gets tough. But there are tools to help us breakthrough blocks and fear and get back on track. I'm going to introduce you to my three favorite tools, and you've probably heard of all of them before because they're effective.

If I can't get the ideas to flow, my first and best method to break through writing resistance is to sit still and allow my mind to empty by focusing on my breath. I find meditation is the best way to begin my writing session, as well as to help me untie the knots of my creative brain so ideas can flow. I've never had a meditation session that didn't elicit at least one idea to guide me out of my writing conundrum. I've even had times when entire parts of a book surged into my brain. For this reason, I always keep a journal handy to write my ideas down before I lose them. I am happy to break out of meditation to write my ideas. I can go back if I wish, or head to my computer to get busy.

If the idea of sitting still isn't appealing, take a long walk. Walking is the second tool in my writing arsenal. I find a long, solitary walk (yes, do this alone) to be as good as meditation for solving writing puzzles. In fact, writing is like piecing together a particularly hard puzzle, and getting outside in nature is a wonderful way to clear space in the brain to see the complete picture of your work.

Journal writing is the other sure-fire trick to unlock my brain and unleash the ideas. Stream of consciousness writing has never failed me. I may not have the entire book plotted by the time I've finished, but I always gain new insight to my work when I take the time to sit down and write without any goal in sight.

For all three of these methods, I specifically begin the process with the conscious thought that I have a writing problem to solve. After planting this thought, I let my subconscious take over.

The sixth writing concept is as important as the other five, but is often overlooked.

THE DOUBLE R'S OF REST AND REFRESH

When you've hit a goal, finished a book, or are simply exhausted, it's time to take a break. Rest is important and can spark new inspiration leading to wonderful ideas that bloom into beautiful stories. In order to make sure you come back to your writing, follow the path of creating a routine and set a limit for your time off.

Ideas abound for rest and refreshment. Treat yourself to a spa day or a day on the beach. Spend time with a good friend you haven't seen in a while. Take a nap or go to bed early. Watch that television show you've been hearing about. Last summer I took a creative writing class. I had recently finished a long and very rough first draft of a novel and I needed a break. I enjoyed writing to the prompts the instructor gave the class, honing my skills without worrying about my manuscript. I tried writing my first mystery story. It wasn't very good, but that wasn't the point. I had fun and gave myself a break before starting rewrites on my novel.

An excellent way to rest and refresh is to travel. I know that travel isn't always the most relaxing of pursuits, but it is restful in that it takes your mind and body to new and exciting places. I often call it "changing my scenery but not my scene" when I think of travel and writing.

Travel is an important part of my life and I've had the opportunity to live in three countries, including the United States, where I was born. I've been living in Ireland for a little over a year now, and every day I find something new in this very different landscape, something to store away for a future tale. My family also lived in India for four years. India offered me vast landscapes, millions of people, and countless new experiences to draw upon for my writing. While it's not always restful, India is colorful, unique, chaotic, and fascinating. India is the main setting for a women's fiction novel I'm currently writing, the overly-long tome I am revising. I love India, especially the way so much is always happening at once.

For another book, I used a shorter trip to Brittany, France as my setting. I took pictures, made notes, and was able to create a novella, the second book in my young adult series.

Take a trip. To anywhere. Visit the next town over from yours. Wander around. Find a cozy café for coffee or tea or eat in a new restaurant. Take a hike along a trail you've never been on before. If you have the time, take a day trip to a new state or region you've never visited. The point is to visit anyplace that's not your normal scene. Let somewhere new fill your senses and your mind with all sorts of possibilities. And take a rest in the process.

My last writing concept, number seven, is to...

ENJOY WHAT YOU ARE DOING

I'd guess that you're like me and writing is something you do because you have to, not because you always want to. Every job can be tiresome, dull, or frustrating. It's up to us to find the joy in what we choose to do.

Gratitude is the best way I've found to magnify joy in all my pursuits. Gratitude is as simple as remembering every day all that writing brings to your life. Be grateful for your creativity. Revel in your ability to paint a picture with your words and delight readers with your stories. Focus on the good your work does to inform, educate, and help others. Be grateful for those who read your work and whose lives you touch.

My hope is that you find some benefit from reading and maybe even implementing one or all the seven steps I've outlined. You may come up with other steps that work even better for you. I'd love to hear them if you do. My wish is that you always find joy and fulfillment in your writing.

ABOUT
KD PRYOR

KD Pryor is the self-published author of three books. She is an avid traveler and, with her family, has relocated several times, including two overseas moves to India and, most recently, Ireland. KD enjoys using travel in her work and is always looking for the perfect setting for the next book in her young adult series. She is also currently at work revising a women's fiction novel set primarily in India.

KD writes non-fiction as Kelley Pryor Amrein. She is an Emotional Freedom Techniques (EFT) practitioner and trained with AAMET. She and a colleague co-authored a book explaining how EFT can help college students alleviate stress.

KD is part of a writing group in Galway, Ireland, where she currently lives, and is also a member of the Women's Fiction Writers Association. Her three books are:

The Portal's Choice (KD Pryor)

The Inn of the Kindred Spirits (KD Pryor)

Tapped Out for College Students: Stress Relief Using EFT (Kelley Pryor Amrein and Becki Stevens)

Visit KDPryor.com to learn more.

9

TO INSPIRE, GO DEEP

SHERRY RENTSCHLER

My desire to write, to create magic with poetic prose, started before first grade. I grew up listening to my mother read stories, and like most children who loved to read, I wanted to create and share stories too. Mine was a happy childhood inspired by characters like Lassie, Oz, and Cinderella; therefore, I wrote about the usual tales including friendships, vacations, and imaginary worlds. There were the obligatory aliens with three-eyed children, duck families who spoke Pig Latin, and later, lovers who lived happily ever after, even with a dragon. I emulated what I'd read and seen without understanding, but then, that is what children do. My stories danced with fun and had eager-to-please heroes and fairy-tale endings. But I was no storytelling phenom, and my poetry and wild fiction—though passionately delivered—lacked the one item required for genuine inspiration: depth.

As I grew up, my writing bloomed with teen angst bleeding out from countless ink pens, wailing over lost loves, failed hopes, and broken dreams. The oh-woe-is-me typical teenager filled binders with broken poems, pages stained with tears, recriminations, and regrets as I emoted the joy of first kisses, ultimate betrayals, and agonized goodbyes. Of course, my teen psyche stressed that no one understood quite as well as I did, no one could imagine the pain as I did. Every teen believes they are the first to know, learn, and experience. Never mind hormones; my emotions overflowed. But for all the feelings rushing through my words, typical or not, I still could not find that missing element that inspired, as I read in others' books.

Eager for validation and praise, I shared stories and over-wrought poetry with my teachers. Truth edged with kindness offered disappointment. Good style, intelligent writing, and budding talent were not enough, they said. My work lacked inspiration. I wrote with passion, but without depth.

What? How could these bastions of knowledge, these educators who taught me to write, not feel what I felt? I shared the truth of my experiences and displayed my feelings like an ala carte lunch platter. How were they not inspired by my joy or touched by my pain? I didn't get it. How deep was I supposed to go?

Years later, while on military leave and visiting my parents, Mother asked about my writing. I shared my successes in journalism and contest-winning stories. But when I lamented over my inability to capture certain awards or to find a publisher, my insightful parent asked me what made my winning pieces different from my other work.

I carefully considered my answer before explaining that when I wrote about freedom or love of country, my words easily leaped from the page; yet other stories failed to garner much notice (unless you considered rejection slips). My sage mother noted, "When you felt passionate about a subject, and you believed in your words, when you wrote with knowledge and understanding, those were the moments you touched others. You have to go deep to inspire."

The simplicity seemed too obvious. Every writer pens about what they know. It is the cardinal rule. We write about what we love. Wasn't this writing with passion? And if you didn't know something, you learned enough to fake it, right?

Then I recalled the words of so many teachers and editors who spoke to me about inspiration. Just being inspired is not enough, they said. First, you must understand your feeling, and then your understanding gives your writing depth. The difference between being inspired and understanding your inspiration is akin to the difference between feeling loved and being in love. That's depth.

> **JUST BEING INSPIRED IS NOT ENOUGH.**

I had forgotten the lessons, believing that shared feelings adequately conveyed my passion. I had emotion, but no awareness.

I thought I finally understood as my writing and my career advanced. I traveled overseas and back, fell in love, married and divorced, went to college and grad school, married and divorced again. I had buckets of inspiration, tons of experience, and an abundance of feeling. However, something in my writing remained out of reach. Despite how I studied and practiced, beyond any beauty and style, somehow I continually lacked the essential ingredient.

I was frustrated, tired of rejection, and ready to abandon my writing. Would I ever understand how to capture this elusive depth?

That's when I had my first epiphany. I was in my early twenties.

Writers and poets know April is National Poetry Month. All the poetry magazines highlighted remarkable poets. Even the trade and technical magazines, which didn't usually print poetry, suddenly filled columns with odd little quotes and dribbles from famous poets. I read them and thought, "They don't understand poetry. This is a ploy, a way to capture that tiny, growing population of dreamers, skeptics, and editors. It's all a kind of ballyhoo because it's expected or required to be profitable and trendy."

I didn't think the magazines understood (or cared) what made a good poem. The choices were often terrible or trite, and I dismissed their commercialism fearing they sold quality for glibness. I preened my arrogance of knowledge believing I understood the bardic way better than these periodicals. Where was this so-called depth now, when the editors chose lighthearted verses over the moving words of the classics?

I lived and breathed verse. I read and wrote poetry every day. I was published in newspapers and small presses, and I scoffed at magazines pitching poetry between their covers just once a year. I shunned people who claimed to have a grip on precision and form, but spent their time reading horror or mystery novels and never actually penned a single sonnet. Yes, I was a poetry snob, and I didn't understand why those more prominent magazines wouldn't publish me. What was I doing wrong?

So, how did the magazines' chosen poems achieve what I labored so diligently to create? Where was this inspiration in all the published mishmash? I showed feeling. I had depth. Or so I thought. What was I doing wrong?

One day I went to my desk and performed my usual ritual pre-poetry writing. First, a little light reading, for inspiration. I'm rather fond of Billy Shakespeare, and on this particular day, I soared through his poetic "Venus and Adonis," taking an hour to study form and style. I scribbled a few ideas until something began to take shape. Feeling pleased, I took a break and read a few magazine articles from published writers. Learning craft is essential.

LEARNING CRAFT IS ESSENTIAL.

Another break for lunch. Finally, I lovingly reviewed a folder of half-baked poems—random thoughts, excellent one-liners, and poesies needing editing—and slaved over a verse. If I worked tenaciously, I believed something beautiful must emerge, and I would swell with pride over the successful creation of a poem. Or so I thought. Until this day.

On this day, I realized it was National Poetry Month, and I was bored with the magazines acting as if this was their greatest discovery. So I shook off the hypocrisy and decided to clear my head with fresh air. Spring was slipping and sliding in the muck that was my backyard, tossing wildflowers between the carefully planted daffodils and tulips. As I walked among them, I smiled at these flowering treasures like poems in the making, random verses just waiting to bloom. Like the blossoms, I believed in my abilities. Suddenly, what once was a dandelion weakly cried out to me. The yellow gone, the gossamer fluff having blown away, there was only a ragged stem. I huffed aloud. A weed! A dead weed among my treasures! Or so I thought. Until this day.

As I stood by that dandelion, a strange compulsion overcame me. I knelt and stretched out beside the lonely stem. I really studied it, surprisingly curious; and then I rolled over in the grass and gazed at the vista observed by this once-yellowed, now empty stem. It had nothing, so why did it cling so tenaciously to the earth, even past its lifetime?

Above me—us—drifted a bounty of clouds in a periwinkle sky, a framework for a nut-brown butterfly cruising close by. The acrid exhaust of a tour bus and fresh grass seed augmented by pungent, wild onions assaulted my nose. Sounds of a bumblebee's deep-rumble and the hollow honking of a geese formation rolled around me on a tickling breeze. The birds sang songs with unknown words, but with melodies somehow familiar and comforting. I smiled, but only because these were "normal things" and not a shock. The hours passed. A grasshopper jumped over me, and I'm sure he was curious about me as I followed his playful bunny-hopping across the errant grasses.

THEN I DISCOVERED TRUE POETRY

Twilight, damp and uncomfortable, covered the strange stem and me. The weed that had thrived on sunshine and wind looked somehow naked and fruitless, limp and alone in a Bermuda yard. I touched the stem, sticky and fuzzy, and understood its tenuous hold in the earth. It was dying. Nothing in Nature seemed to care; not a bird or even a worm paid attention. Yet this little stem clung in thirsty desperation to a sandy, unyielding soil, staring like a silent guardian at its last night sky. There was no arrogance or sorrow, but easy acceptance. Above, a vista of stars and a universe beyond it were unreachable to this weed, yet it sang with the totality of life. It loved the earth, even as it faded.

Amazed, I remained with the barren stem until the morning dew draped us both; the once proud yellow stalk now black and dead. I had spent the night in wonderment of a simple weed. This, I finally understood, is poetry. This was depth.

I rose from the earth, body cold, but heart exploding with awareness. I knew I would return to my writing exercises, read a few trade magazines, and hunt out the obscure poetry obligingly pigeonholed between recipes and editorials. I decided to review a few works by some unpublished friends who believed they had uncovered the secret of poetry. Intrigued as never before, I didn't discount them and wanted to hear their stories.

Later, as I pondered a fresh dandelion—all yellow, full of promise, and holding court on my desk—I shed my arrogance. Instead, I wrote humbly while in the company of the dandelion because it was April and National Poetry Month. And because, unlike my peers, I never really understood poetry. Until this day.

Such was my first epiphany and how one single day changed my writing. That deepening awareness in the life and death of a little weed opened my mind and demonstrated what I was missing all these years. Poor dandelion was more than "just a weed" or "a simple flower." Here was the missing piece. I felt the lesson.

My work improved, but I sensed it wasn't enough. Years later, I had my second epiphany; a harsher lesson.

Both my parents had pets when they were growing up, and they extolled the virtues of a furry friend. They gave me a puppy when I was two, but someone stole it. As a teenager, I had a tiny turtle. He didn't last long because he was hard to pet. I promised myself that one day I would have a dog or cat, a buddy on whom I could lavish all my excess love. However, I was unprepared when a cat came into my life, all black fluff and wide amber eyes pulsing with curiosity.

Born on Halloween, my new kitten was a jolt of pure magic in my life, so I named her Magic. I also called her my butt buddy because she was a cuddler who snuggled at my hip. We were friends for over 13 years.

Together we managed two moves, two apartments, one townhouse, and one home, two fireplaces, numerous boyfriends, one divorce and one new beloved husband. Through every moment, my little Magic taught me what selfless love was, how to give love with my whole heart, and what grief felt like when you loved with all your soul. Animals have remarkable depth; raw, unfiltered and generous.

When people tell you that their animals are family, like children, it is true. My Magic required boundaries, teaching, grooming, and attention as if she were a child. And like a child, she required constant watching and consistent loving. Hale or sick, she depended on me to be there, and I was. She knew what she wanted and demanded affection. But she gave back that love and attention in spades with extra cuddles and an intuitive nature that defied logic.

Animals are passionate about everything, and they teach you to share this passion, engage in life, and demonstrate your love. This opening of one's heart is the beginning, and it's discovering the real passion behind love. Unconditional love is both scary and uplifting, but animals give love freely and teach us how to give in return. They don't understand "tomorrow." For them, there is only now. That is their awareness.

My lesson—the epiphany—and understanding didn't hit me until the day Magic died. Sick with kidney problems, the time came when it was kinder to euthanize her. I couldn't imagine a life without Magic. I feared the coming emptiness, but I hurt too much to keep her alive and in pain. Burning tears stung my face as I held her head and looked straight into her eyes while the drugs filled her body. I whispered my love and prayed she understood me as I watched the light leave those great black pupils. It haunts me to this day. When heart shattered and grief overcame me, the epiphany happened.

Love and hate, life and death, joy and grief are the masters of our passion and inspiration. What gives them truth is the depth we allow ourselves to feel, and what we give back. Grief, like love, isn't for the dead, but works for the living. Grief taught me how to say goodbye. The love I felt because of Magic, taught me how to love a human being in a genuine way I hadn't before her. Depth comes from experience and from being open to any all-painful truths. Raw, unfiltered and generous, like Magic.

> # WITHOUT DEPTH, PASSION IS NOTHING MORE THAN A THOUGHT.

Passion is often a word used when describing inspiration. Without depth, passion is nothing more than a thought, or even a dry emotion. To write words isn't the same as feeling them. To feel them is only the beginning. To know real inspiration is to be able to share the depth of each feeling, to wrap yourself in the world, with an awareness to become a part of it. This depth gives stories resonance and power.

Knowing your passion is how you inspire. Inspiration with depth is how you touch your readers. The emotion underlying everything, the feelings that complete the whole, this is where truth waits for the writer and what every reader craves.

Be brave and determined to learn more than what passion is or what inspires. Go beyond the knowledge into the *how* and *why*. Discover the broader emotions. Bring depth, and your stories will shine with a brighter light filled with more profound feelings.

I've had two distinct realizations. One of love, found in the scope of life, and one of death, found in the breath of love. The two spectrums are what allow me to share the best of who I am as a writer. More aware than ever, my goal is to share these lessons when I write.

If my mother were still alive, she would ask me how my writing is going. Today I might tell her that I succeeded, and perhaps brag a little. I achieved my goals, both in publishing and in winning that previously eluded recognition. I would undoubtedly add how much I love what I do because I'm aware of how blessed I am. She might give me a very knowing smile with a mischievous twinkle in her eye when she replies, "That's deep, Sherry."

I hope she's right, because inspiration, whispering in my soul, beckons me onward.

ABOUT

SHERRY RENTSCHLER

Sherry Rentschler is a best-selling, multi-award-winning, multi-genre author, and writing coach. A retired U.S. Air Force non-combat veteran, Sherry completed her bachelor and graduate degrees while serving her country. Her background includes bylines in newspapers and online journals, plus previous work as an assistant poetry editor and photojournalist. Shery was featured in *Southern Writers' Magazine* and *Focus on Women Magazine*, and has been a guest speaker on numerous radio shows (*The Ron Shaw Show, La Femme de Prose, Off the Chain, Authors Corner* and *Hangin' With Web Show*).

Sherry's latest release is a paranormal romance, *Love and Blood*, book two in the "Evening Bower" series. Amazon dubbed the first book, *Time and Blood*, as a bestseller.

Her causes include the National Network to End Domestic Violence, as well as programs to end bullying like StopBullying. gov. Sherry is also a strong advocate of Smile Train (seeing children get corrective surgery for cleft lips and palates), Stand Up 2 Cancer, and youth literacy programs.

Sherry's guilty pleasures include indulging in fine wine, dark chocolates, and old B&W Sherlock Holmes movies. A recognized vampire scholar and dragon collector, she and her husband live in North Carolina.

10

YOU ARE A CREATOR

BONNIE G. HANSON

In my earliest memory of being aware of my desires, I was filled with an immeasurable love for horses and an equally urgent need to create. I simply arrived on the planet with this love and a knowledge that these two elements of the universe were a part of me, encoded in my DNA. It was inevitable that both would play a significant role in my time here. After years of visualizing my imaginary stable playmates, my horse materialized when I was 11 years old. We were comrades for nearly a decade, and shared magnificent experiences together each day and while competing in show events. We were natural companions and it came as no surprise to me when I later learned that horses are highly intuitive animals. We were very connected, like best friends, and had fun competing with some of the best riders in the state. It would not occur to me until later in life how powerful visualization can be.

Creating was the same as breathing for me, and took many forms in my early years. At ages four and five, I was playing music on my play-by-number organ (my feature song was, "Home on the Range"), painting wooden Christmas ornaments at the kitchen table, and learning to cook and create decorated desserts and cookies with my Mom. Later I would graduate to decorating custom cakes, composing endless photographs with a variety of cameras, documenting my (horse) life and love for landscapes. I enjoyed painting ceramic figures, and made my first business selling painted and beaded jewelry.

My grandmother Maxine enhanced my cooking skills and taught me to crochet snuggly blankets. I loved cross-stitching meaningful creations (mostly animals) and gifting them to family and friends. Music was always present, as my organ later gave way to the clarinet, and then the flute, which later propelled me into an international concert tour. If I wasn't playing tunes, I was certainly listening to music at every opportunity. Today, the camera on my phone allows me to document life at a moment's notice, to capture a gorgeous sunset; and the opportunity to play and paint, stitch, craft and decorate still brings a profound satisfaction to my soul.

CREATION IS PART OF THE SOUL AND COMES IN MANY FORMS.

Creation is part of the soul and comes in so many forms. Simply lean toward what moves you and experiment with it. Allow the beautiful journey to unfold. Leave your need for perfection by the wayside and allow yourself to dabble and play. Allow yourself to be inspired by your life.

The beauty in creating is the joy we feel when we align and connect with our souls and allow that soulful expression to rise to the surface and physically come into being. We can experience a true sense of aliveness when we allow the depth of our truth to surface as we align with our desire and passion. The true prize is to then share our unique creations in the world and touch other souls with our perspectives.

Writing came fairly easy to me in grade school and beyond, although I never considered it a pleasant experience. I suppose it was the many reports, which I painfully procrastinated on that made it feel unpleasant. The dreaded creative writing time in class usually left me staring at a blank sheet of paper

> THE TRUE PRIZE IS TO TOUCH OTHER SOULS WITH OUR PERSPECTIVES.

and longing for some type of instruction on what exactly the teacher wanted me to write. Now, in my adult years, writing has become my latest mode of creation. I've used it as a tool to overcome fears and to heal hurts from the past. Writing has been a profound conduit for connecting with people and has paved the way for some incredible, life-long friendships with other creators. Maybe I have more perspective to share after 50 than I did at 15, or perhaps it was finally the right time to write.

My favorite way to get into the creative flow of writing is to connect with nature. Being in the park surrounded by trees or on the beach next to the crashing waves provides a profoundly grounding feeling for me. Often, I will stroll on the beach, picking up trash (loving the earth) and recounting, then releasing the to-do list of thoughts of the day. Snapping a few photographs of my surroundings begins the creative process and provides satisfaction and enjoyment for me. When I reach the halfway point of my destination and head back to my starting point, I just allow myself to be open and listen for whatever thoughts come up.

It's quite like a walking meditation. The first half of the walk I am releasing what's on my mind and then continue walking quietly and listening during the second half of the journey. Usually, this feels like it creates open mental landscape for good ideas or thoughts to come in and congregate. I use the microphone on my phone to capture my notes as I continue to walk and to think and to allow. When I return to my car, I review my photos and hydrate. It's quite a magical endorphin rush that is fulfilling in so many positive ways: being outdoors (usually in the sunshine), exercising, loving the planet, releasing and processing concerns, creating photographs and capturing good ideas.

> # CREATE A ROUTINE THAT IS GROUNDING TO YOU.

Create a unique routine that is grounding to you and opens a channel for your creative thoughts. To paraphrase the words of the great Wayne Dyer, "Inspiration is simply to be in-spirit". Connect with what feels good to you and allow what feels good to come out from within you.

TIPS FOR MAXIMUM CREATIVITY MINDSET

- Play, experiment, and have fun!
- Create for your own personal joy!
- Immerse yourself in the environment that lights you up! This will be where you feel relaxed and free and open to receiving inspiration (the beach, the forest, a quiet morning or night, in the shower).
- Focus on your "deservability": You are here for a reason. Your voice is necessary.

- Allow yourself to release any resistance you may have about being judged or liked. Shift your focus to remember that you are remarkable! You are more than enough. Your creation is worthy.

- Sharing your creation is the icing on the cake that brings a new layer of satisfaction to all who enjoy it.

- You and your creation will not bring satisfaction to everyone. Stop trying to please everyone and have fun with those who connect with your unique expression. The joy is in the journey.

ABOUT

BONNIE G. HANSON

Bonnie Hanson is a Certified Professional Coach, and CEO of Hanson Plumbing. Her passion is writing and making a difference in others' lives. She is the mother of four children. Bonnie lives by the motto; "It's not a question of who is going to let me, it's a question of who is going to stop me."

11

TOOLS, HABITS, AND STRUCTURES

LINDA JUVALD

Compilers' Note: This author's work uses UK spelling to keep
consistency with the rest of her published works.

Writing my first book has been one of the most fantastic, gratifying and amazing processes of my life. It has also been one of the hardest, most frustrating and challenging adventures I have ever embarked on. And if it is your dream to write a book, I recommend with my whole heart that you go for it.

For me, one of the key motivators to keep going through the ups and downs of writing a book has been the knowledge that I can help many people by putting my knowledge and experience into a book. This is such a gratifying feeling and is part of accomplishing two major goals in my life; helping people living happy lives and helping humanity and earth to move up into a higher frequency.

I am an avid reader, an expression that I like a lot more than the "whale reader", which I heard for the first time recently and which is apparently used by Amazon in some connections. I love books, both fiction and non-fiction. And whenever I want to learn how to do something, I turn to books first, and then to webinars, online courses, and such.

As a book lover, it has been a lifelong dream of mine to write a book, and 2018 was the year for that dream to come true. So following my standard operating procedure when starting out on a new venture, I turned to books first, and some of the best ones I have found so far have been the *Books for Writers* series by Joanna Penn. They are awesome; practical, technical, funny and personal all in one. I am learning so much.

Now with all that in mind, consider my wild joy when I had a chance to become part of this anthology, which is designed to inspire other writers to keep going and fulfil their dreams of writing and being published. It runs in my genes to want to help other people reach their goals—whatever they are—and in the process helping them become happier and more balanced.

I will share with you my own journey, the best tools I have found, and the habits and structures that helped me reach my goal of publishing my first book in 2018. My next book is already outlined, and more titles that are just now on the idea level are so going to happen!

PREPARATION

Preparation is crucial for success when setting out to achieve a major goal like writing a book.

Several areas of preparation helped me achieve this lifelong dream. They are:

- ✎ Finding your big why and goal-setting
- ✎ Researching and learning
- ✎ Preparing yourself and your workspace
- ✎ Preparing to write the book itself

I will go through each one below.

FIND YOUR BIG WHY AND GOAL-SETTING

I suggest that the first step towards actually achieving your goal of becoming a writer is to discover your big why. This is important because your big why will help you to keep going when it feels like it is never going to happen.

One way to do this is to go through the values process, which will help you become really clear on what is important to you. This will inspire you and help you in the process of putting your big why into words. Going through this process will help you prioritise the tasks that are most important for you and will also assist you in making better decisions in all areas of your life.

Ask yourself: Why do I care about this (writing the book or any other project you are starting out on)? What is important about it? Why is this specific project important to me? What is the motivation behind the project? How does this project touch my heart?

> # WHY DO YOU CARE ABOUT YOUR WRITING PROJECT?

Couple that with the big rocks goal process to make sure that this goal (in this case writing a book) is really one of your big ones. Since you are reading this book about inspiration for writers, it probably is! Buckling down and getting clear with yourself about this goal, both in terms of motivation and in making sure that it aligns with the most important values in your life, will help you tremendously along the way.

You can find information on both the values process and the big rocks method in my book *Manifesting Happiness*. Other great resources for finding your big why are easy to find by doing a search or hiring a coach. It is also a good idea to use the SMART method to reach a clear and motivating phrasing of your goal. There are many good resources on the internet on the SMART method.

This entire part of the process will help you get into the right mindset to really believe you can do this, because now you just have to focus on your goal and take things one step at a time. And when the going gets tough, you can easily refer back to your big why and your values.

RESEARCHING AND LEARNING

If there are aspects of the writing process that you are uncertain of, please do some research at this point. Learn about the things that you need to know in order to start—or continue—writing. However, be very conscious of using your time wisely at this point. Do not spend your time researching marketing methods if you have not yet started your book. Writing the book must be top priority. Also, if you need to do research about the topic of your book, this is where you would start doing that as well.

PREPARING YOURSELF AND YOUR WORKSPACE

> SETTING UP YOUR WORKSPACE MAY BE ENORMOUSLY IMPORTANT.

For some people, setting up their workspace is enormously important. For others, not so much. In order to discover what is important for you concerning a well-functioning workspace, I recommend looking at how you function best workwise. Are you most focused when you work in a specific place? Is it conducive to your productivity that your desk is clear? Or do you love to work in a café? Some people really love the hustle and the bustle of a café, but when they look at the number of words written during a café session as opposed to an office session, it turns out that they are actually more efficient in the office. And for others it is the opposite.

So getting to know yourself as a writer is important. Start noticing how you behave in different settings and when you feel the most satisfaction after your writing session. And also start tracking your numbers. How many words did you write today? Where were you when you wrote them? How long did it take you to write them? There is gold in knowing these things.

Maybe you think you already found the best way to write—which is really great—but I still urge you to try out different settings and test produced word count vs time spent to find out what works best for you, before you settle into a specific place or rhythm for good. You may be surprised.

PREPARATION FOR THE BOOK ITSELF

For me, one of the most important preparations for writing the book itself is the creation of an outline. To prepare the outline, start with a brainstorming session. There are many different ways of doing this, but one method I have found to be most efficient is mind-mapping. You can do this either with pen and paper or electronically, whichever you feel comfortable with, or within Scrivener, using the corkboard feature (more on Scrivener later). Other people use index cards or sticky notes, which they can move around as the structure appears during the brainstorming session. Whichever method you use, this step is crucial, and I highly recommend using a mind-mapping method for both longer and shorter projects.

I always find that even though the brainstorming session is invaluable and makes writing so much easier, I invariably end up remembering things along the way that I somehow didn't remember during the session. I get inspired as I write, which is absolutely a positive sign. I simply add whatever it is to the cards or sticky notes and move on from there. I have also found along the way that some sub-chapters, or maybe even main chapters, have to be switched around for things to flow in a logical order. This is just a sign that the book or writing project is evolving into the best version it can possibly be for the reader.

MY BIG WHY

I believe I can help change the world for the better by helping individuals change their lives. That is a powerful motivator. And this is one of the things that carries me through when I think of stopping. I consider the benefits that people will get from reading my books and blog posts, and how that will then carry over to other people, moving further and further out in larger and larger circles of influence. It's such a fantastic and vivid image in my mind.

This gets me out of my own comfort zone and motivates me to move beyond my boundaries. Then I hold the contemplated action up against my core values to make sure that it does not violate one of them and that I am actually okay with it.

One of my big sources of inspiration are my coaching clients. Hearing them work through the process of reaching their goals, working with them to overcome their obstacles (be they big or small), and the inspiring and oftentimes inventive ways they find to make it work for them inspires me greatly.

It really makes me happy when I get to be part of their lives. This is especially the case when they experience a light-bulb moment, take that first exciting step toward their goal or when they reach it. That incredibly wonderful energy in their voice is beyond rewarding and gets me so excited and feeling very grateful.

I have always loved coaching and helping people make changes in their lives, and this made a huge difference for me when I decided to write my first book. Becoming clear on this big why and making sure that it aligned with my core values meant that I could couple my coaching experience with writing from my heart. It enabled me to help people move from feeling frustrated with their lives to feeling more in charge, and was incredibly motivating and rewarding to me.

Oftentimes in the writing world I hear the question: Should I write something that will sell and make me money? Or should I write from my heart? My clear take on this is; if you are writing your first book, definitely write from your heart. Write the book that is in you and has just been waiting to come out. The motivation and drive to keep going that you will gain from this is invaluable.

Now, don't get me wrong. There is nothing, absolutely nothing, wrong with wanting to make money. It is after all a prerequisite for surviving in this world. However, if that is your primary or only goal, what comes out of you will likely not carry the energy and passion that I am sure you would like. Write about things that you find interesting and that you believe will make a difference in a reader's life. This goes for both non-fiction and fiction. However, you need to follow the path that you feel is right for you.

> FOLLOW THE PATH THAT YOU FEEL IS RIGHT FOR YOU.

MY BIGGEST CHALLENGE

The main challenge for me has been to overcome my very introverted nature and dare to put myself and my name out into the world. And even though writing a book has been a lifelong dream, knowing my name would be "out there" was a big obstacle to me.

I have used quite a number of tools to work my way through this issue. Working with my coaching clients on their challenges and hindrances, and being so inspired by their solutions, has been instrumental in moving me to follow my dreams. Added to that, I have used the personal development tools and the trainings I went through over the years, like becoming a Certified Advanced Ho'oponopono Practitioner, working with the Sedona releasing method, and NLP, for instance. These have all been instrumental in venturing out on the journey towards being a published author. Being willing to look at my own patterns and work on changing the limiting beliefs I had around being published changed the journey for me entirely.

And you know what? It turns out that most people are very supporting and encouraging and very glad to have your help to improve their lives bit by bit and make their day a little brighter. This goes for both fiction and non-fiction.

So, if you are in that place where you feel like you are holding yourself back because you are afraid of the visibility, please keep going. Examine the beliefs you have about yourself as an author, and then look for evidence that these beliefs are wrong and start looking for evidence that supports better beliefs about yourself.

I also researched how other introverts deal with this issue and discovered that it is a matter of overcoming fear through action. To quote a book by Susan Jefferson: "Feel the fear and do it anyway", and then discover that you actually lived through it and feel better for having done it. For many introverts—me included—it is a matter of dipping your toe in slowly, doing smaller things. And then repeat and repeat and repeat. Over time this strategy also leads to slowly choosing bigger impact tasks.

Keep your big why and your values visible and let them inspire you to get you through the hard days; days where it feels like you will never reach your goal of becoming published one way or another, days when you wonder why in the world you thought you could do this. Trust me, you can! Work on yourself so that you can pull out those motivating reasons when you are down.

Another motivating method I use when things just don't seem to flow, is to read about and listen to other people who have done it. Encourage yourself with stories of people who went through the whole process before you and not only survived, but who are now thriving and living the life of a writer that you want so much. Read about the things that got them through the hard times and be inspired by their stories to keep going.

MY WRITING RITUAL

My writing ritual tends to change over time, and some steps disappear as new ones appear, so for me this is more of a dynamic process than it is set in stone.

At the moment, I write during the morning after a 15-minute ho'oponopono meditation ritual. This makes me feel clear-minded and motivated and starts off my writing session on a higher note.

Furthermore, while writing I listen to ho'oponopono "clearing music" to keep me focused. I find it helpful to use the same piece of music to start out a writing session, and I am building a writing playlist so I can just keep going without handling the music along the way when that piece stops before the session is done.

Before starting a writing session, I make sure that I have water and tea available. I also make sure I have some fruit or nuts handy as well. This way I will not have to interrupt my writing if I get hungry during my writing time.

I often use the essential oil rosemary for concentration or a fresh plant that I can touch and smell, or I use the essential oil lavender if I feel like there are stresses in my body before I get into writing. Other good essential oils to use are orange or tangerine, which helps energise you.

If I have limited time, I will set a reminder on my telephone to stop and get ready for the next thing in my calendar. If I am lucky enough to be able to choose to continue writing for quite a while, I just let my creativity run for as long as it feels right.

At the moment, I have the privilege of being able to follow this process on most days. However, all days are not alike, and sometimes my well-made plans fall to the wayside, crushed by urgent matters that I simply have to deal with. And there are other times in my life when a morning writing session is just not an option. So be flexible and do not let anything keep you from writing.

I like structure and thrive with rituals like the ones described above. I have, however, also discovered that the more I work on my writing, the more inspiration I seem to receive during the day and not just during my designated writing time. I find myself suddenly writing quite a few words during the evening because an important thought struck me that just had to be written down right away. Or maybe I am waiting at an airport someplace, and inspiration strikes. Becoming less rigid in my rituals has given me so much freedom to just write when I feel the urge and simply cannot help myself.

> ## LET YOUR INTUITION SHOW YOU THE WAY.

My suggestion is to develop your own ritual and stick to it as much as possible. This is most likely the most efficient writing time you will have. However, be flexible and do not let it stop you if your day gets messed up and you are unable to write at the time and place you usually do. Let your intuition show you the way, and when inspiration strikes do whatever you can to start writing right there and then.

TOOLS AND TRICKS

For me, the one thing that truly changed my behaviour in terms of writing was acquiring Scrivener. It is a powerful tool, and the word count bar changing from red to yellow to green as I work toward my daily writing goals is the most amazing motivation; very simple, yet so effective.

Setting a writing goal is, of course, paramount in order to use this as a motivational factor. There are many different suggestions out there recommending how to set your writing goals. Many believe in setting a goal that stretches you, like setting the daily word count goal quite high. This is another one of those things that you will have to test until you find out what your sweet spot is to actually reach it most of the time and still be challenged to get as much done as possible in the time you have.

For me, however, it has turned out that setting the goal quite low has really worked. A very low daily word count has meant that I can meet that goal most days, even on days that are really busy or on those off-days where nothing seems to go my way.

I have also discovered that knowing I only have to reach a low number of words to get a green day, gets me started on days where I know a higher word count goal would have made me feel like not starting at all. In the end I usually end up writing a lot more words than the word count goal once I get started.

Now, to get back to Scrivener, I must say that the easy way I can write an outline on the corkboard and move chapters around if needed has been a game-changer for me. I use this as a mind-mapping tool and regularly go to the corkboard view to get an overview of where I am in the project and what my next task is. In other words, I highly recommend Scrivener.

I started out using Evernote, which is also an amazing tool, and I use it for many, many things. But it was not a life-changing tool for me as a writer, and I struggled to actually produce words with it for quite a while. As I mentioned, switching to Scrivener did the trick for me.

Of course, you do not have to use Scrivener to get the green light as a motivating factor each day. You can also use a big old physical calendar where you mark all the days you achieve your daily goal with a green marker. You will be amazed at the efficiency of this simple technique. As your green streak becomes longer, you will definitely put in a lot of effort to keep that green streak going.

The next really important tool for me has been a course called "Learn Scrivener Fast", by Joseph Michael. There are three different levels of this program and you do not in any way have to invest in the most expensive one. Just start with the lowest or the middle package. Read through the description and find the one that appeals to you. The value here is inexplicably high, and you can always upgrade later if necessary.

As far as both information and motivation goes, the *Books for Writers* series by Joanna Penn, as also mentioned earlier, are superb.

I am on a continuous journey to find good tools to increase my efficiency, both overall and in connection with writing, and I have therefore tried quite a few efficiency-increasing tools; for instance, using the Pomodoro method, which is quite often recommended to writers. I know a number of people for whom this works like a charm, but this is not good for me. It does not feel right to me to stop writing just because the 25 minutes are up and an alarm goes off. Especially not if I am in the flow and I have the time available.

So I return to the tool that seems to work the best for me (at least so far), which is using a daily word count. Scrivener is a fantastic tool, as I can see the word count bar moving from red to yellow to green. Very cool.

This just shows that there are no hard and fast rules on how to become most efficient as a writer and what will trigger you to act and to keep going. There are many really good tools to help you improve, and ultimately you will simply have to try out a few of them to find one that works well for you.

Your current time situation is, of course, an important factor when you choose your method. If you work full-time, you may want to use the Pomodoro method for just one round every day as your daily writing goal instead of a word count goal. This would be considered a great success if you are writing in your spare time.

CELEBRATE AND RECHARGE

Be sure to celebrate your wins along the way. Here are some examples from my own celebration and reward plan: I give myself 15-minutes of quiet time with a good cup of tea every day that I reach my daily word count goal. During this time I do absolutely nothing except enjoy my tea. This means no computer, no telephone, and no screen of any kind. For every seven green-light days in a row, I give myself time to read just for fun for at least one hour. For every finished large project, we go out for lunch and spend a few hours just hanging out and enjoying life.

I believe that celebrating and rewarding yourself is a key factor to success. Time off to let yourself just relax or do something that is fun and enjoyable for you is so important for you to succeed with your writing, and in fact with any other project in your life. If you do not make sure that you recharge your own batteries at regular intervals, you will burn out. And that would put an effective stop to your endeavours to reach your goals.

And it turns out that taking time out of a busy schedule

> **TAKING TIME TO RECHARGE WILL MAKE YOU MORE EFFICIENT.**

to recharge when you need it will actually make you more efficient when you return to your work, and you will end up getting
more done than if you push through and don't give yourself time
to recharge.

Therefore, take time off and celebrate your achievements along
the way.

Whatever you do, do not give up. Keep going toward realising
your dream of being a writer. Do the work to find the structures,
tools, methods, and the time that work for you. And keep taking
one step after the other.

Read about the fantastic tools and methods all the other writers
in this book recommend and use. Test them and find the ones that
work for you. And skip the rest. Trust your own sense of what
resources are good for you.

ABOUT
LINDA JUVALD

Linda Juvald is a transformational life coach and author of *Manifesting Happiness: Transform Your Life from Frustrated to Empowered.*

Linda has worked internationally with HR, recruitment and administration within the corporate world for many years, using coaching extensively throughout that time. She has furthermore worked as a life coach ever since her certification as an NLP Coach from ITS in London in 2004, as this is where her passion lies. In early 2017, Linda decided to follow this passion and start her own coaching company; "Leading Edge Creation Ltd."

It is Linda's deep inner passion to assist others in gaining clarity in their lives and fulfil their dreams. She loves supporting people in discovering their true passion, reach their goals and support them in navigating through the abundance of choices and opportunities that life constantly throws their way. Being empowered to make choices that are right for each individual invariably changes lives for the better.

If you would like to work with Linda 1-on-1, please go to the website to find the details on how to do so.

Visit www.leadingedgecreation.co.uk to learn more.

12

PARALYZED BY PERFECTIONISM?

AN AUTHOR'S GUIDE TO USING GOALS TO OVERCOME YOUR PERFECTIONISTIC TENDENCIES!

DR. SUE MASSIMO

Your deadline is just around the corner. You've been working on your writing project for quite a while now but can't get past that one part. It's just not coming together as you think it should. You know you should just sit down and finish it...now!

But the little voice in your head is telling you that you can't just do that. You can't force it out of your head or just crank out anything to complete the project, even though you know you have to get it done. You can't do it; it's not perfect yet.

Well, now you definitely can't concentrate. Instead, you'll take a minute to quickly check your emails (as there might be something important that needs attention) and you may as well see who's on Facebook. There might be training you should watch, as you surely don't want to miss out on that next "shiny object" that could propel you or your work into the stratosphere. Maybe you'll play a quick online game, as that always puts you in a good mood. Plus, another cup of coffee will give you more energy so you can get back to working on that project.

You know you're passionate about your writing and it's something you really want to do, but find yourself dreading it. Plus, that deadline is still looming. Perhaps you got an extension and moved the date again. Or even better, you gave up on having a deadline altogether, so now you are experiencing the "someday syndrome" where you keep telling yourself that one of these days you'll finish that article, book, poem, or play.

Well, we've all been there—at least many of us have—and more times than we would like. If this scenario resonates with you, ask yourself a few questions. As an author or writer, have you ever felt that:

- You're consumed with writing your best, but it's never good enough?
- You'll let down your readers if you don't produce quality work?
- Even though you give 100%, the results will never meet the standards of others?
- You delay the completion of projects until everything is just right?
- You spend hours on details that should have only taken 20 minutes?
- You're paralyzed by your perfectionism, leaving you drained and never satisfied?

Probably for many of us, somewhere along life's many roads, we became critical of ourselves and our work. We looked to others for approval and to validate our accomplishments, and set high standards for ourselves, patting ourselves on the back for exceeding them. Then life got more complicated; we had more responsibilities and set even loftier goals in an attempt to be successful. Now we find ourselves frustrated, stressed-out or anxious, realizing we haven't enjoyed many of our accomplishments along the way. In other words, we were trying to be perfect.

Well, if any of this resonates with you, then you probably know there is a term for people just like us, and that is being PERFECTIONISTS. That's not necessarily a bad thing, as some qualities may be advantageous in certain circumstances; but for most, your perfectionistic attitudes have been getting in the way for quite a while. So, now is a perfect time (no pun intended) to put your perfectionistic tendencies aside and open your mind to discover a world of endless possibilities, untapped talents, and accomplishments with a realistic view of reaching the meaningful goals in your life.

To understand more about these perfectionistic tendencies and how they may be affecting your writing, let's look at some different types of perfectionism that you probably didn't know existed. Then we'll discuss the continuum of perfectionism and whether it can be an asset or not. The vicious cycle of perfectionism will be presented, as well as strategies to break it. Finally, we'll explore how the pursuit of goals, crafting your goals, and defining a vision for your writing and personal life can help you adopt a healthy mindset to beat perfectionism. Hopefully, these strategies and exercises will ultimately lead to you begin the challenge of over-coming your perfectionistic tendencies so you can realize your ultimate vision as an author.

TYPES OF PERFECTIONISM

Let's briefly look at the different types of perfectionists and some new thinking around the construct. According to research, there are three types of perfectionism that stem from the orientation in which it manifests. The first group is self-oriented perfectionists who hold high standards for their performance, are conscientious, and are productive and successful in their careers. Socially-prescribed perfectionists feel pressure from others to be perfect in everything they do, and often tie their self-worth to standards prescribed by others. Lastly, other-oriented perfectionists tend to hold others—like family members and colleagues—to very high standards, resulting in being critical and judgmental of others' performances.

According to some newer theories, perfectionism can be in the form of adaptive or healthy, and maladaptive or unhealthy, constructs. There's nothing wrong with holding high standards for your work and being somewhat of a perfectionist. The adaptive perfectionist strives for success, but adjusts for their strengths and weaknesses. It only becomes a problem when holding oneself or others to unrealistic expectations or feels like everyone around them expects the best of them. Often, the maladaptive perfectionist avoids projects due to their fear of failure, feels the pressure from outside influences, and experiences stress and anxiety, which can be detrimental to their mental health.

IS PERFECTIONISM AN ASSET OR A DISADVANTAGE?

Many people experience perfectionism on a continuum, so our tendencies lie somewhere along the line, depending on specific circumstances, situations, and events. In this manner, perfectionism can be both an asset and a disadvantage for writers in a variety of ways. Many qualities, like striving for success, can be advantageous for authors to a certain extent, but often become detrimental in their excess. On the positive side, perfectionists tend to be highly motivated with a strong work ethic. They typically enjoy their work and are committed to their goals. They want to be the best and they work hard at it. They are coachable, with a desire to learn and improve their craft almost to a fault.

Conversely, perfectionism hurts their ability to create freely and confidently, usually due to incredibly high expectations for their work. They tend to lack trust in their skills and often have fragile self-confidence. They do not accept mediocrity and often worry too much about what others think of their work. While striving to be perfect, they quickly become frustrated with making mistakes, which may lead to becoming anxious and stressed. Ultimately, this is all equated with the fear of failure.

In today's society, perfectionistic tendencies are often mistaken as precursors to success, but as we've discussed, they can be detrimental to achieving it. Now, there is nothing wrong with pursuing excellence in any endeavor, but the difference lies in whether you are driven to success, as seen in perfectionists, or you have a strong drive to be successful. The perfectionist is driven by goals beyond their reach and a desire to be perfect which robs them of the self-satisfaction of realizing their dreams. Successful individuals work towards their goals and dreams, have realistic plans in place to achieve them, and are personally satisfied with their accomplishments.

> # PERFECTIONISTS OFTEN SET THEMSELVES UP FOR FAILURE BEFORE THEY EVEN BEGIN.

THE CYCLE OF PERFECTIONISM

A vicious cycle of perfectionistic tendencies is often set in motion through striving for goals. Perfectionists are committed to their goals and will work diligently to achieve the outcome. Having goals may seem like a great idea, but without the proper guidance on how to create and monitor their goals, perfectionists will often set themselves up for failure before they even begin.

To start with, in attempting to be successful and perfect, perfectionists tend to set impossibly high goals, although they aren't aware of it at the time. Often their expectations and over-emphasis on "shoulds" and "musts" serve as rules for how they are supposed to behave or what they have to accomplish, and are the driving forces of their goals. These goals rarely account for the perfectionist's true desires, as they are too consumed with external expectations of what they believe others expect of them.

The next phase of the cycle is inevitable, as perfectionists start to realize that they are heading towards failure. Besides their goals not being reasonable, they probably weren't based on the desires of the authors, who are starting to feel the effects. Unfortunately, you can only work so long toward a goal before it's obvious that it's out of reach. It's challenging to work hard to reach goals if they don't come from a place of deep passion.

The third phase of the cycle is where productivity starts to wane as the perfectionist tries to be the best at all times. As goals aren't met and deadlines are missed, the writer becomes less effective and off task. The usual orderly and organized life of the high achiever begins to crumble as the realization of producing a masterpiece is unlikely. The perfectionist often engages in a rigid type of thinking about their work, so if it isn't perfect, then it must be terrible.

The last phase of the cycle is a mix of fears and doubt, making mistakes and inadequacy. As the perfectionists aren't reaching their lofty goals, self-defeating thoughts and behaviors emerge and the fear of failure begins to manifest. The fear of making mistakes keeps writers from truly releasing their creativity and realizing their potential. They begin to doubt their talent and writing and believe if their work isn't perfect, they've been defeated. Failure to achieve their goals becomes tied to their self-worth and self-esteem, and this is where the real breakdown

> # IF IT ISN'T PERFECT, THEN IT MUST BE TERRIBLE.

begins. By this stage perfectionists are caught in a trap, feeling like they will never be good enough. From here the perfectionist may abandon their goals altogether or unfortunately, reset their goals to ones just as unattainable as before, thus setting up the same old self-defeating cycle.

IT IS POSSIBLE TO CLIMB OUT OF THE SPIRAL.

If this describes you, never give up. With a little effort, it is entirely possible to climb out of the spiral of perfectionism and leave the cycle behind you. Your productivity will increase and you'll be completing your work while feeling good about yourself in no time!

HOW TO USE GOALS TO BREAK THE CYCLE OF PERFECTIONISM

Perfectionists tend to be highly organized with countless lists of things to do—including setting goals—but here is where the problems begin. Unfortunately, perfectionists aren't very good at goal-setting because they are striving for perfection. Their goals are usually out-of-reach, unattainable and not enjoyable. So, the true perfectionist will love the idea of this exercise, but will cringe at the thought of shifting away from being perfect to being practical, pursuing excellence realistically, and focusing on the process rather than the outcome. It all takes some real shifts and adjustments in mindset so the perfectionist can learn to set, achieve, and enjoy pursuing their writing goals now and in the future.

Let's take a look at the science behind goal achievement and how to create and set your goals. First, we need to discuss an essential topic underlying your goal-setting endeavors, and that is your "why." Why are you are setting these particular goals? Why are you pursuing them? Are they for yourself or for others?

YOUR FUTURE SELF—WHAT IS YOUR VISION/DREAM FOR YOUR LIFE?

Ask yourself what your vision or dream is for your future. What are the dreams and goals that are unique to you, your business, writing, and personal life? Ask yourself what provides purpose, passion, and happiness in your life. What are your strengths and weaknesses? Are you pursuing your potential?

Look at the many areas of your life and dream of a future perhaps of being a successful author; financially secure, physically, emotionally and spiritually fit, and having healthy relationships and quality family life. What does it look and feel like? Why do you want to do it?

When it comes to perfectionists, they are often stuck in the pleasing-others mindset. This isn't a healthy mindset because the individual needs approval from others to validate their work, as well as their worth as an individual. Rarely do perfectionists base their goals on their true desires and wants, so they rarely feel any joy if they happen to achieve them.

So, for this exercise think of yourself and not what others expect of you or what others are doing. If you had to summarize your vision or dream in one sentence, what would it be? Can you narrow it down to one ultimate goal? Can you write it out as a vision statement?

Now, underneath your overall life's vision, where does writing fit in? Is it paramount to everything else, on the back burner, or somewhere in between? How passionate are you about your writing and how much happiness does it bring you? Are you realizing your potential as an artist? If not, that's fine for now, but is this something you truly want to pursue? If so, then writing may provide you with a sense of self-satisfaction that may be lacking in your life as of yet.

This time, if you had to summarize your "writing" vision or your dreams as an author in one sentence, what would it be? Can you narrow it down to one ultimate goal? Can you write it out as a vision or goal statement? Visualize what that would look and feel like. Keep your overall and writing visions in mind when determining the goals you'll be creating and setting for your next writing project.

THE SCIENCE BEHIND GOAL ACHIEVEMENT

A recent study looked at how goal achievement is influenced by putting them in writing, committing to goal-directed actions, and being accountable. Here are three tools which should be a part of everyone's goal setting strategies and the reasons why.

✒ Goals Must be Written Down

"Ink them, don't merely think them!" These six words represent the motto I've used for decades when it comes to goal-setting. The human brain interprets the act of writing differently than it does merely typing on a computer. The answers are found in the neurological sciences, but primarily, the act of writing sends impulses to the brain which increases learning and memory.

Research into goal achievement supports the effect of writing down goals. The study found that those who wrote out their goals as opposed to those who did not, accomplished significantly more. In fact, the act of writing their goals resulted in an increase of 50% in reaching their goals versus those who didn't write them down.

✒ Goals Require Commitment and Action

The study also looked at people who not only *wrote* their goals, but made *action* commitments. The participants who sent their commitments to a friend (considered a public commitment) accomplished significantly more than those who just wrote action commitments or didn't write their goals at all. The study also showed that making their goals public resulted in reaching 64% of those goals as opposed to making only 50% of their goals if they made action commitments but didn't share them with anyone.

✐ Goals Require Accountability

In the study, some of the participants were asked to send a progress report to their friend on a weekly basis, in addition to the action commitments. The study found that this group accomplished significantly more than those who just formulated action commitments and those who sent their action commitments to a friend. Plus, the group that sent progress reports to a friend achieved 76% of their goals overall! That's the kind of results we all want to have, right?

READY TO TAKE ACTION?

So, are you committed to your goals? Are you going to take action? Are your reasons strong enough to make that commitment? Hopefully, your answers are "Yes!" First of all, you must write down your goals. There are two ways to be committed; one is to take your goal-directed actions and keep them to yourself— like so many perfectionists—and the other is to make your goals public by sharing with a friend or colleague. Sharing is your next step, and it's a "must" for the perfectionists.

If you take it a step further and have an accountability partner who not only knows what your goals are, but holds you responsible for those goals, you can achieve even more. This might be a friend, but it may be better if they are going through a similar situation to yours or have similar goals. An accountability partner can help hold you responsible for accomplishing your goals.

Perfectionists need accountability partners too mainly because they tend to want to do everything themselves. Plus, they often don't tell others about their goals because of the shame they feel when they don't meet them. You genuinely need support with a dose of tough love thrown in to keep you on track; so reach out and connect with an accountability partner. Now let's take some action and set some goals.

CREATING S.M.A.R.T.E.R. GOALS

If you haven't had much luck in meeting your goals in the past, you may need to make them SMARTER. Most all of you have heard of SMART goals, and this is just a variation on the theme as they represent the fundamentals for you to follow when formulating your goals. Keep in mind, that these goal-setting techniques supplement the realization of identifying and fulfilling your long-term goals and ultimate vision for your writing and personal life.

Here are the fundamentals of SMARTER goals to use to help you create goals that are precise, motivating, challenging and doable, all leading you to realize your full potential. Think about the ultimate goals you are contemplating for your writing and overall future self. As you read along, refer to your writing vision and focus on one goal, preferably a small one to begin with, such as writing an article for your blog or a chapter for your book that represents a piece of that ultimate vision. Then jot down your primary goal and add to it and revise it as each strategy is discussed.

A word of caution here for perfectionists. Make sure you don't fall into the trap of setting goals you think others expect of you, and for the extremely detail-oriented, try to refrain

> DON'T SET GOALS YOU THINK OTHERS EXPECT OF YOU.

from turning this exercise into another masterpiece. The idea is to have the big picture in your mind, but to identify one aspect that would fulfill one part of that vision. Part of the exercise is to get you thinking in terms of the stages or steps that need to be taken to satisfy that one goal. Remember, these aren't set in stone, as they will probably need modification over time, so for this exercise just start with one goal.

S—GOALS SHOULD BE SPECIFIC

Goals should be clear, precise, and specific. Now is not the time to be vague, uncertain, and guessing about your goals. Ask yourself what steps, tasks, and mini-goals need to be accomplished to get closer to reaching your vision or your larger goal. Then, break it down into manageable pieces and stick with it. Don't skip over any parts, and make each piece the next logical step in a sequential manner. Imperfect goals will get imperfect results. Likewise, unclear goals lead to an unclear future, which is undoubtedly not what you want.

Since the perfectionist tends to look at the outcome, it is imperative that every larger goal is broken down into many pieces even baby steps. As one goal is reached, set the next one just beyond the last level of accomplishment. Strive for clarity and specificity in your goals, and never underestimate the power doing so may have in your future.

M—GOALS SHOULD BE MEASURABLE

It's important to have measurable goals so you can track your progress and keep the momentum going. Often these goals use actual quantitative and quantifiable measurements using money, time, numbers or weight to name a few. As an author, you'll use measurements such as word count, number of pages, and time spent writing. It's essential to have a baseline from which to measure, so before you get too excited, record where you are currently so you'll see the slightest of improvements. For perfectionists, this is particularly important because they tend to think in terms of the outcome instead of determining where they are currently or anywhere along the continuum.

Most of your goals will encompass physical measurements, but the emotional and spiritual goals you'll want to consider are subjective. For many of you, these may include goals of focus, motivation, or spiritual connection. Monitor them like any other goal and because it is your feelings of accomplishment that matter. The great thing is that *you alone* are the evaluator of these types of goals. It is still a good idea to set a baseline predicated on your feelings—perhaps on a continuum—so you have some form of an objective evaluation. Measuring and assessing progress helps you to stay focused, meet your deadlines, and feel the excitement of getting closer to achieving your goals.

A—GOALS SHOULD BE ATTAINABLE

As a perfectionist, you'll want to refer to this section often in creating and staying on track with your goals. Attainable goals are challenging and achievable, as opposed to overwhelming and unobtainable. This doesn't mean they are easy to accomplish or readily within your grasp. On the other hand, goals that are set too high or are clearly not in reach are not realistic. Unrealistic goals may be emotionally challenging as well, where fears, doubts, and uncertainty may manifest. Rephrasing them into positive goals and attainable objectives can keep you on the edge, but not over the edge of your comfort zone.

> KNOW WHAT IS WITHIN YOUR CONTROL.

A certain amount of personal judgment is involved, and this is another area that can be difficult for perfectionists. You must consider what is within your control and what is not. Very often the outcome of a goal is unknown. Make sure you factor in variables such as resources, training, time, and financial constraints. For example, if you're contemplating a long-term goal that may seem unattainable, try to map out the steps you need to take to aspire towards that goal. If you do, it will be motivating, challenging and achievable. If not, look at ways to change the goal so there are several milestones to achieve along the way, resulting in attaining similar goals as well.

R—GOALS SHOULD BE RELEVANT

All your goals should lead to your ultimate personal vision in life which includes your writing vision. Most importantly, they must be *your* goals and not those of others. So, as you set your daily and weekly tasks and goals, you always want to ask yourself if they align with your vision.

As you pursue your goals, it's inevitable that a variety of obstacles will get in the way. External influences, as well as internal feelings, affect everyone, not just perfectionists. Sometimes the barriers affecting you are because you set a goal with lofty expectations or they aren't relevant to your true vision. Feelings of fear, doubt, and making mistakes will affect your progress. Remind yourself of your vision and reach out to your accountability partner for support.

Other obstacles that affect your goal attainment are events and people. They may appear to pull you in all directions, but hopefully you will be able to refocus and forge ahead because you have your vision in mind. As you set your goals and as circumstances arise, ask yourself if doing those "other" things are really in your best interest and support your ultimate vision for your life. If not, learn to graciously say no. If the answer is "Yes," then go for it!

T—GOALS SHOULD BE TIME-BASED

All of your goals need to have a deadline or target date, so you have something on which to focus. When you are creating your goals, look into the future and determine what you need to accomplish along the way to meet that goal. Break down your vision and long-term goals into manageable objectives, keeping in mind the time constraints that may be placed on them. Use your calendar to set a target date for a project then work backward and set dates for the list of tasks or mini-goals you'll need to reach along the way.

Here again, perfectionists need to be very objective, realistic and honest with themselves when establishing these times. Perfectionism can rob you of time because you might spend hours working on one detail when it should have only taken 15-20 minutes. You'll also want to plan for the amount of time each component of the goal should and might take and try to stick to it. As you move forward in your schedule, block off times that are needed to accomplish the amount of research, writing, and editing that you will need to reach those mini-goals. In general, remember to set realistic timeframes for smaller goals that will eventually lead up to accomplishing your final objectives.

E—GOALS SHOULD BE EVALUATED

Evaluating your progress and checking off your goals is a useful way of confirming what was accomplished and what you need to do next as you pursue your vision. Your goals should be reviewed and tracked daily, weekly, monthly, seasonally and yearly, depending on what you're focusing on at the time. That may sound like a lot, but once you create and establish the goals, you only have to revise them as circumstances arise.

As a perfectionist, it's important to focus on your progress and not on the final outcome or achieving perfection. Take time to reflect on what worked and what didn't and make adjustments. It's a great time to acknowledge your mistakes and learn from them. Your work shouldn't be divided into successes and failures—as you tend to do—but should encompass the small goals you accomplished along the way.

R—GOALS SHOULD BE RECOGNIZED & REWARDED

Keeping your goals laid out in front of you or on your home office or workspace wall and seeing your progress is both motivating and satisfying. As you fulfill your goals by taking action steps, even baby steps, you are making progress; and before long, you'll complete an entire project, eventually leading you to realize your ultimate dream. Recognize that achievement and reward yourself for your effort and hard work as you reach these milestones!

Celebrating your accomplishments, no matter how big or small, will help keep the momentum going and your vision goals within reach. The reward is especially crucial for perfectionists who often don't enjoy the process leading up to the final goal attainment and rarely congratulates themselves on their work. The journey toward your goals should bring pleasure, not just when the end result is achieved. That's why it's important to reward yourself during the process of completing your goals and mini-goals. You determine your own reward system, but remember to praise yourself as you accomplish milestones to realizing your full potential.

FINAL THOUGHTS

The idea behind this chapter was to provide a glimpse into the world of the perfectionistic author and those struggling with perfectionistic tendencies. Some of you may have recognized the traits associated with the three types of perfectionists. As you've probably surmised, many of us experience the problems associated with perfectionism, and some of us are spiraling downward in its cycle. One way to help break the cycle was discovering your "why" in what you are doing in your writing and even your life, and establishing goals to help you realize your potential. Getting the most out of your goal-setting efforts is paramount to achieving your dreams and now is the time to make sure you are using the proper fundamentals to craft your goals.

As with learning any new skill, certain principles of setting goals need to be followed and practiced to get the most from this kind of activity. Creating SMARTER goals along with writing them down, committing to them and being accountable on a consistent basis also sets the stage for realizing your full potential in your writing and personal life. Setting goals in life shapes your dreams, provides a focus for behavior, and supplies you with the ability to act on your desires, as well as handle obstacles in your way. Goals give you permission to reach, change and grow in new and exciting ways to better yourself and the lives around you.

> # SETTING GOALS IN LIFE SHAPES YOUR DREAMS.

Hopefully, if you are a perfectionist or feel you have perfectionistic tendencies, you'll try some of these suggestions to avoid their potentially paralyzing effects on your writing and personal life. Eventually, you may come to realize how your perfectionistic tendencies are hindering your everyday life in a multitude of ways. As you begin to think in alternative ways and your mindset begins to shift, you'll start to feel better about yourself and achieve more than you could before. As you stand up to perfectionism, you can succeed in the pursuit of excellence in a healthy manner. Remember, abandoning your perfectionism is something you'll never regret.

Author's Note: If you feel you or a loved one is experiencing the paralyzing effects of perfectionism, please reach out to your local mental health professionals and consult with a clinician trained in the treatment of perfectionistic behavior.

REFERENCES:

Hewitt, P. L., & Flett, G. L. (2004). Multidimensional Perfectionism Scale (MPS): Technical manual. Toronto, Canada: Multi-Health Systems.

Matthews, G. Study Backs Up Strategies for Achieving Goals. (2015).

http://www.goalband.co.uk/uploads/1/0/6/5/10653372/strategies_for_achieving_goals_gail_matthews_dominican_university_of_california.pdf

Rice, K. G., Richardson, C. M. E. & Tueller, S. (2014). The Short Form of the Revised Almost Perfect Scale. Journal of Personality Assessment, 96(3), 368-379.

ABOUT

DR. SUE MASSIMO

Dr. Sue Massimo is a co-author of hundreds of articles and three books in her field of Sport and Exercise Psychology. She is a former competitor and elite-level gymnastics coach, and now a Mental Game Coaching Professional. Her Best-selling co-authored book, *Gymnastics Psychology: The Ultimate Guide for Coaches, Gymnasts and Parents* consistently ranks as an Amazon Best Seller since being published over six years ago.

Dr. Sue primarily works with athletes to help them proactively prepare for competition by discovering the mental and emotional challenges that will likely affect their performances. Dr. Sue helps them learn strategies like goal-setting and life skills to overcome those challenges and implement a mental game plan to help them realize their peak potential in sports, school, and life.

Whether you're an athlete mastering your skills for competition or an author writing your next book, the premise of using proper goal-setting to help overcome your perfectionistic tendencies is the same.

Visit SuperstarMentalGames.com for more.

13

FULL CIRCLE

KATHRYN RAMSPERGER

I really wanted to be a pediatrician. It was my mother who first told me I needed to be a writer. As I grew, my teachers all agreed with her. When I heard that people could be both doctor and scribe, I relented, and my writing journey began at the tender age of 10. I've been a researcher, a communication specialist, a humanitarian, a manager and director of international communication and publishing departments, and a coach. Yet through it all, I've never been able to walk away from writing. It's a thread that runs through everything I do. I'm compelled to write.

Even though I've tried to run away from it a few times.

And what I didn't realize until the past decade: I've healed people even though a D in chemistry and a C in geometry kept me from a perfect high school GPA, even though I didn't get a full scholarship to University of Virginia, even though I never held a stethoscope to a child's chest. I've healed them through my words.

Even though Mrs. Covey in fifth grade agreed with my mother about my potential, my soul didn't embrace their urgings until I entered middle school and picked up a copy of the November

1970 *Reader's Digest*. The magazine featured famous people writing about *why* they read and wrote. It was a brilliant idea that attracted my attention in a way a conspicuous ad would have failed to do. It might have been the first form of content marketing. I still have it pasted into my 70s scrapbook:

> "The secret of happiness," declared the English novelist Norman Douglass, "is curiosity." He lived to be 84, doubtless helped along by his endless curiosity." So quoted news commentator and world traveler Lowell Thomas.

At 12, I hadn't had nearly enough time to satisfy my own inquisitive senses. I expected to be at it for many more years, but I was amazed that instead of "killing the cat"—as I'd been taught every time my curiosity had put me between a rock and a hard place—curiosity could make you *happy*. My curiosity was actually a good thing.

CURIOSITY CAN MAKE YOU HAPPY.

I read on. Thomas felt that curiosity was satisfied through travel.

It was tough to research back then, but I found other articles by and about Lowell Thomas in *The Reader's Guide to Periodical Literature.* He was one of the first travel writers, he knew Lawrence of Arabia (having met him in the Middle East), he was sent to report on war and wilderness by U.S. Presidents. He was a famous newscaster and broadcaster. (He was also, by the way, a shameless self-promoter, which is why I happened on his *Reader's Digest* blurb that was full of other people's quotes from the public domain.)

From that time forward, I was hooked. On happiness as the key to health. On travel to faraway lands. On Lowell Thomas. On the Middle East. On writing.

Also in 1970, through what I now know to be synchronicity at play, I saw a New York Times article titled "Death Comes To The Peregrine Falcon." It was all about the very last living bird of its species (not in captivity). Encroaching urban areas and the pesticide DDT had put the final nails on this already rare bird's coffin.

I followed along with the peregrine's precarious journey until 1979, when another was released from captivity and took up residence on a Baltimore office building roof. Flash forward to today, and this falcon, the world's fastest diving bird, clocking in at 188 miles an hour, is no longer facing extinction. It was taken off the endangered species list as the new century dawned.

THAT'S WHAT WORDS CAN DO

I found out about the peregrine falcon through journalism, and it's my belief the bird was saved because of the attention these articles drew. That might have been the moment I decided to become a journalist.

I took a high school journalism class later that year, the same year I began watching television journalist Ann Compton anchor our local news. I was fascinated because I'd never, ever seen a woman anchor the news. Ann Compton went on to be a renowned national broadcaster and White House Correspondent. She, too, placed another writing flame within my heart and soul because she was there when I needed her direction.

I WANTED TO SHOW JOURNALISM WHAT A WOMAN COULD DO

These writers and more, without ever meeting me or speaking with me, directed me toward what would become my career and life path. For instance, I read Eudora Welty's story "A Worn Path" and Annie Dillard's *Pilgrim at Tinker Creek*. Both independent, gifted, feisty women had ties to Hollins University. So had Ann

Compton. I decided to attend Hollins, and I sat at their feet as they read. My advisor and mentor was none other than Annie Dillard's ex-husband, Richard Dillard, a talented author and poet in his own right, and perhaps the best teacher I've ever encountered.

As I waited for my college acceptance letters, I read Khalil Gibran's *The Prophet* almost every day. His philosophy and faith were profound, and he was one of my first peeks into the Middle East and its culture. It was he and a few other personal friends that catalyzed my award-winning debut novel, *The Shores of Our Souls* 40 years later, after having written four previous (as yet unpublished) novels, the first of which was at Hollins.

Writers like these taught me structure, voice, and persistence. Persistence is the most important quality a writer can have. It's the collection of their works long after their deaths that keep their words alive, but most (Dillard being the exception) did not get immediate attention. They just kept on writing, and in those days, you had to have a patron or other connection to find a publisher. We're much luckier these days; it's the best time for a writer in the publishing arena... ever.

FIRST, YOU NEED TO PAY YOUR DUES

I went on to publish news and feature stories for local newspapers, hold cue cards and do production work for a local television station, and research—then write—for National Geographic publications before freelancing for Kiplinger. All the while submitting to literary journals and poetry anthologies and receiving many more rejection letters than acceptances. All along with the dream of being a published novelist someday.

Moving on to the International Red Cross & Red Crescent, I facilitated workshops in Africa, led crisis communication teams during the first Gulf War and the early years of HIV/AIDS, and developed training on the Geneva Conventions. I then went on to head its publications department. I've traveled to every continent on the globe except Antarctica and Australia, and I've written some of my most intriguing thoughts on planes and trains or hiking in the wilderness.

"We do need to bring to our writing, over and over again, all the abundance we possess," said Eudora Welty in her seminal work *On Writing*. In fact, the people who inspire me most are the people I write about because they compose in large part the abundance of my life. Here are the two people who have remained with me in spirit, to give you two excellent examples.

I interviewed Randy in 1988. He lived the first part of his life in a family riddled with addiction. He married, had kids, divorced. At a time when Waterloo, Iowa's two major corporations were laying people off, and when 6,000 people abandoned their homes leaving their keys on the mantels for mortgage companies, Randy started shooting drugs. He became the county's first AIDS case. He told me about the bullying his daughter faced, how he wasn't allowed in neighbors' homes, and how former friends were now afraid of him.

Randy joined, then led, an AIDS support group. "I've always bitched about how nobody jumps in to help," he told me. "So I jumped in myself. I've got a good year left in me." Randy led the support group nine more months. His mom read the story I wrote about him at his funeral. Randy's style of support group is now used globally. People with HIV are more accepted today, but despite education and support, 1.8 million people became newly infected with HIV in 2017. Around 1 million people died from AIDS-related illnesses that same year. I write for these people, and I write for Randy.

I met Sally this year. I don't even know her last name, and I might never meet her again. She's a writer just like me, but what I didn't know until the end of our conversation in a healing group was that her life had been similar to mine. She, like me, had to confront her own mortality at an early age. She'd had a near death experience, and I'd had a brush with death when I contracted melanoma and a couple more times when I hemorrhaged. She'd lost friends and family members to mental illness and suicide, just as I had. But she didn't tell me any of this until she'd listened to my loss, to my grief. And that made me connect with her all the more. She knew what I'd been through. That's why I write: so that we may all walk in The Other's Shoes.

I wrote about Randy, and I am writing about Sally.

> # I WRITE TO CONNECT PEOPLE WITH EACH OTHER.

I also write to connect people with each other, to share our joys and our pains, to illustrate our similarities instead of our differences. I write for the young woman vendor in Bcharre, Lebanon who told me I had beautiful eyes. I write for the cab driver in Marrakech who would not allow me pay him the same rate the Mercedes drivers were charging. I write for the young children who made it over the border out of Rwanda only to die of machete wounds in the refugee camp. I write for the female market owner who taught me how to stay healthy in Africa, and for the Kenyan of Indian descent who healed me with herbs and began my journey toward holistic healing. I write for the homeless Brooklyn crack addict who invited me into her room at the shelter, for the single mom who always makes it to blood donation to remember her family members who died of leukemia, and for my two writing soul sisters who passed over the last decade. I write for humanitarians, like my dear friend Nancy Beaudouin, who put their lives on the line every day to save just one more life. I write in their honor and to show that we're all one. I write to share their stories, and I write to share my own story. *Because we are our stories.* And our stories will save the world.

Nearly all my ideas come while I'm traveling or in the shower, many while showering in hotels. And all my writing led to my novels, though I couldn't see it at the time.

The day I started walking toward a published novel was September 11, 2001. I was freelancing and writing business reports for nonprofits when the planes hit. It was my son's first day of public school in the DC suburbs. The next week, I knew what I needed to write. I wrote *The Shores of Our Souls* in less than a year. Revisions took much longer and finding an agent even longer than that. The first in a trilogy, it was published traditionally in August 2017, a year before my 60th birthday and the year my youngest child graduated from high school.

You can do all this, too. You just have to 1) begin; 2) persist; and 3) believe in yourself. You can write a novel, but there is so much more in life that can use your words and voice, philosophy and perspective.

Writing touches everything I do, including (and maybe even especially) my coaching. I've been a master intuitive and creativity coach for a decade now. When I coach, I heal with my stories and my words. My clients share their stories with me, and they journal. They free up their souls, and that frees up their creativity. When I write, I shine a light on suffering and injustice and show readers what they can do in some small measure to help.

Are you a writer? Probably. Anyone who wants to connect their thoughts and feelings with someone else, even if it's only themselves, is a writer. It's the best form of healing available, and it can heal the world--if the world is ready to truly read it. My intention in writing is to educate

> **WRITING IS THE BEST FORM OF HEALING AVAILABLE.**

and inspire, but I get healing for myself, too. I find out a lot about myself by writing about others.

My love of the word, my love of people, my love of travel, my love of the natural world, my infernal and incessant curiosity—they all led me to where I am today. And in the words of another great writer, the poet Robert Frost, "I took the road less traveled by, and that has made all the difference." Most writers look for their own path. They think outside boxes, boundaries, and labels. In learning about others, they find themselves.

Fast forward to today; I've been able to view some peregrine falcons. Two falcons nested on the Maine cliffs, and more recently a few on trip to Iceland. We stood fascinated with a large group of onlookers as they soared above us. The birds were majestic in flight, and graceful as they flew back to their roost. We realized they were safeguarding their nest because of fledglings. I've read that peregrines are nesting in cities all over the world now. They've found their way with a little help from their friends, especially the writers that made their cause public.

Is writing and publishing a difficult road? Absolutely. Don't let anyone tell you anything to the contrary. Is it the best job? Maybe. It has been for me. I have traveled far and never, ever looked back. My life has come full circle. I'm a healer and a writer. And I have so many more words to share with you.

SIDEBAR: YES, YOU **ARE** A WRITER

I'd love to give you some inspiration to begin your first book or dig the one on your zip drive back out. Here's what I've found that kept me going through tough times (including the transition from print to digital books).

- Remember it's all about the story. It's not about you. It's not all about how many books you sell. It's not entirely about the reader. If you allow it, your story will tell itself.

- Use other forms of arts media to inspire you as you write: a photo, a piece of music, or even another author's words. If you don't know what to write next, get up and draw or finger paint on an easel. Then come back and write refreshed. Try writing with a pen instead of a keyboard.

- Make sure you exercise, especially if you're stuck. (I need to remember this one myself when I'm on deadline.) I continue to find some great stories on daily walks.

- Ask other people for their stories. Keep them in a journal. You never know when they'll come in handy. Write down the way people speak and snippets of conversations. It'll help you write dialogue.

- Don't throw anything out! I won an award for a story I recently published that had received numerous rejections in the 1980s. Scan if you must, but don't burn your novel in a moment of angst. Everything has its time.

- Seek the community and mentorship of other writers. With the internet you can easily find your own Lowell and Khalil.

- Never give up! Persistence is key in writing and publishing. Don't settle for less than the right fit either. I had over 200 rejections from agents on my novel, before finding one that said "yes" and who loved and championed my book.

- Have fun! That's what *The Cat in the Hat* tells us: "It's fun to have fun, but you've got to know how!" When you find yourself getting too serious, find a joke, read a kid's book, or better yet, read a kid's joke book to a child. Laugh, especially at yourself. Then keep on reading and writing!

ABOUT

KATHRYN RAMSPERGER

Kathryn Ramsperger's literary voice is rooted in the Southern tradition of storytelling and is informed by her South Carolina lineage. She began her career writing for *The Roanoke Times* and *The Gazette* newspapers and later managed publications for the Red Cross and Red Crescent in Geneva, Switzerland. She has contributed articles to *National Geographic* and *Kiplinger* magazines. She's been an intuitive life coach and creativity coach for a decade.

Writing from a global perspective, her themes are universal, yet intensely personal and authentic. Winner of the Hollins University Fiction Award, Kathryn is also a finalist in the 2018 Faulkner-Wisdom literary competition. *The Shores of Our Souls* won a 2017 Foreword Indies award for multicultural fiction and also won an America's Best Book Award. Kathryn has traveled to every continent except Antarctica and Australia and worked in Europe, Africa, and the Middle East.

A graduate of Hollins University (Roanoke, Va.), Kathryn also holds a graduate degree from George Washington University. She currently lives in Maryland with her husband. She's mom to two young adult children and two spoiled felines.

Visit shoresofoursouls.com, groundonecoaching.com, or check out her eBook *The Novel Life* for more.

14

WRITE...
IN SPITE OF FEAR

KRISTEN JOY LAIDIG

I was about six years old. I had a tiny pocket notebook and a pencil, and I was overly obsessed with lizards. It was the first story I ever attempted to write. It was a weird fictional non-fiction blend (back then I didn't know the full difference) and filled with facts I found in the encyclopedia, as well as examples from my personal experience with the creatures. And when I found it later in life it was absolutely the most horrible thing I'd ever read.

Yet that childhood memory of writing in that little book every evening for several weeks straight is one of my fondest. I can only hold on to the belief that the fondness I feel for that experience is due to the path it set me on toward becoming a writer; not the story that never saw the light of publishing (for good reason). From that early age I was bit by the writing bug... and I would never be satisfied without writing as part of my life ever again.

My inspiration for writing has shifted throughout the years. While I never considered myself much of a fiction author, I found myself writing a science fiction novel during chemistry class in high school. My teacher knew what I was doing and gave me permission to write during class, as well as a sneaky way to get away with it. (Hey, I was the teacher's pet.) Fourteen chapters later I set that manuscript aside to focus on college.

BECAUSE... PASSION

I took one creative writing class in college and loved it. However, having experienced my hopes and love of a passion being crushed by professors in the tightly-run, limited-sight institution of university, I knew if I pursued writing at that level I would lose my creativity, passion, and love for the art. So I kept my degree focused in another area and quieted the incessant voice inside that urged me to write. It was a daily struggle, even with assignments that required me to write about a specific subject... usually one that I had zero interest in.

My passion for writing smoldered under the surface of my conscious mind, just begging to be let out in a more creative way than the university allowed. I was afraid. My body trembled as I entertained the idea of becoming a real, published author. And then after graduation I was approached by someone to help start a publishing company, which involved creating my own first real, published book. When I let that tiny bit of my writer-self out to play, it started a torrential downpour of love for the art and for other writers. It was as if the one stone from the dam that had been holding my writing dreams back broke loose, tumbled, and the rush of excitement and energy blew past the dam into my consciousness and out the tips of my fingers onto the computer screen. It was captivating and addicting, similar to the "runner's high" experienced by athletes. And in that moment, I knew I had to have more.

That experience and the act of finally opening myself up to the possibility of writing being a foundational part of my life, led me to create and build the internationally-known and award-winning brand *The Book Ninja* to help other authors experience this euphoric journey. (I realized I'd hit the "big time" when my brand was mentioned on the TV sitcom *Younger*... LOL)

And yet building that brand wasn't enough. It wasn't enough that I also built a companion award-winning blog full of helpful articles for authors. It wasn't enough that I'd authored over 36 books. It wasn't enough that I created journals, coloring books, cookbooks, planners, and author's guide books. It wasn't even enough when I poured my heart out in my soul-filled book *Asskickonomics* and its companion workbook and journal. It wasn't enough that I embraced my creative writing side and published my first children's' book *The Last Dinosaur*. And it wasn't enough that my best friend and cohort in writing came up with the idea to create a supportive environment for writers and hold free weekly writing dates through a new partner brand, *Writing is Art* (WritingIsArt.com).

No, as soon as I started to embrace my inner writer, my blog flourished as several of my posts went viral. My writing became deeper. My friends noticed. More doors to success began to open.

And because I just couldn't stop the floodgate of new ideas, I asked Natalie to partner with me to create an entirely new series of books, beginning with this one that you're holding in your hands. Because to write means to shine part of your soul on another. It's vulnerability at its core. It's intimidating and sometimes downright horrifying. It's an exposé of your soul to the reader. So sometimes it's easier to accomplish in partnership rather than on your own.

> TO WRITE MEANS TO SHINE A PART OF YOUR SOUL ON ANOTHER.

Yet even in the lack of partnership, we writers are *compelled* to act on our desire to keep putting words to the page. To keep spreading our messages. To keep telling stories. Because, like me, at some point in your life you poked the dragon inside. You pulled at that stone that was holding back those floodgates of passion. You experienced the energetic rush of ideas that you just *had* to get down on paper. You discovered the power of words to change yourself, to reach others with new ideas, and most of all to quiet that voice inside that screams, "Write, already!"

BECAUSE... THERAPY

So I write because I must. I don't write on a schedule or time-line, but rather what I prefer to call "batch" writing. I'll get hit with inspiration or be motivated by something someone posts on Facebook. That smack upside the brain will ignite an idea that grows under the surface of my mind and eventually matures into patterns, words, thoughts, sentences, and paragraphs. I get emotionally charged when I'm angry at an injustice, such as if one of my consulting clients is dealing with a time-sucking vampire who only wants to pick their brain for free. If it's a line that is crossed, or even just danced around, I get energized to write about it.

Most of my writing these days is emotion-driven. I don't believe in what's taught by so-called gurus in the publishing industry that you should find out what's selling and write about that. Who cares? What if you hate that topic? What if you don't want to write steamy romance, but you have a passion for historical creative non-fiction? What if you really don't want to write about vampires even though that's the trend? I feel that while you might make money by following trends, it's not sustainable. Because writing is about more than just what's "hot" on the market. It's about what will sustain your soul. Writing will always be a part of your life. If all you do is chase down the shiny, trendy objects, you'll never tap into the true power of writing. The investigation of your own self. That piece of yourself you're afraid to expose, yet know you must.

This is why writing is, in fact, one of the deepest forms of therapy that exists. Whether you're writing your personal story (which is obvious that you'll be exploring the depths of your own mind) or a fictional account of a wayward bounty hunter in another galaxy, all writing contains pieces of your personal experience. The emotions of your characters are often based on experiences you've had in your own life, as well as the lives of those close to you. In fact, it's said that the best fiction is based in reality. Poetry is often the lamentation of a life struggle or proclamation of a forbidden love. Children's book stories often come from tragic experiences in your own childhood. Blog posts are often explorations of deep thought, experimentation, or a call to support a cause. Virtually every form of writing exists as a part of you exposed in the form of words on a page or screen. And every form of writing demands to analyze a part of yourself. Some piece of you that makes you "tick." Your innermost thoughts, fears, struggles, and stories of overcoming... your *self*.

BECAUSE... TRUTH

Writing exposes the truth about *you*. It's an outlet for your innermost thoughts and ideas widely accepted by society. It's a relatively safe way to engage others, especially if you're an introvert. And yet at the same time it sometimes feels like the scariest thing in the world. Because at the end of the day, all writing does one thing. Fiction, non-fiction, kids' books, articles, poetry... they all expose a truth. It could be a truth

WRITING EXPOSES THE TRUTH ABOUT YOU.

about an idea, a concept, or a scary truth about yourself. A truth about fear, anger, or love. Your truth, their truth, and absolute truth. No matter what, writing exposes some sort of truth.

The scariest truth-writing exposé is that truth about yourself you try to hide deep inside, away from prying eyes. And yet when you write, you're able to expose a facet of that truth in the form of presenting new thoughts, ideas, and even characters' stories. Think about some of the most powerful writing you've ever read. Your favorite authors. One of my favorites is the famous novelist Ernest Hemingway. He described the truth that appears in writing well when he said;

> "From things that have happened and from things as they exist and from all things that you know and all those you cannot know, you make something through your invention that is not a representation but a whole new thing truer than anything true and alive, and you make it alive, and if you make it well enough, you give it immortality."

This idea that writing is immortal is sure to contribute to the fear writers often have of exposing those inner truths and creating something new. Because writing really is around long after the author has departed the planet. Often, what we learn from past, now extinct cultures, is from the writings they left behind. I'm continually fascinated by the idea that in order to leave knowledge of how things are now to future generations, we must somehow make ourselves immortal. And immortality through writing is both exhilarating... and terrifying! That means long after you've left your words on a page or screen, future generations may discover those words, and like quotes by famous now-dead authors like Hemingway, those generations' lives may actually be changed.

What a responsibility. No wonder fear holds the writer back more than anything else. The writer is literally putting their heart and soul out into the world for eternity. For future generations to be inspired, motivated, and in some cases angered. To be judged… forever. And that is the truth. Your writing *will* be judged. Your published words, whether on a blog, as a book, or part of a larger work such as this one, will be immortally condemned to judgement from readers.

YOUR WRITING **WILL** BE JUDGED.

If you as a writer are not at least sometimes fearful, there's honestly probably something wrong with you. Every writer experiences fear. It's a normal part of the process. If you didn't, I'd be worried because you wouldn't be writing your truth from your heart. And that is a disservice to the position of "Writer," because your writing should always include some portion of your truth. Your *self*. Your soul. Only then is it worth the risk of judgement to push past the fear and write.

BECAUSE… BREATH

My good friend Therese Sparkins once gave me a phrase to hold onto in my darkest, most fearful times, and today I'm imparting that wisdom on to you. She said, "Fear is excitement without the breath in it." Think about that. What do passion, fear, and truth all have in common? The potential to be combined into an energy that can drive your writing for years. It's the pent-up force inside every successful writer that just has to be let loose in order for them to breathe. It's the excitement behind the fear.

Therese's wisdom has stuck with me for years. In and of itself is proof of how words that impart a truth can change someone's life and give them an insight that applies to almost every life situation. It's a simple sentence that could be worked into any genre of writing. Read the following sentence again, then close your eyes and really *think* about it. "Fear is excitement without the breath in it." I could write an entire book about how this combination of eight simple words has changed my perspective on every fear I face.

Writing is often accompanied by fear. And equally as often it is charged with the energy behind excitement. Yet the two—fear and excitement—are brothers. They are intertwined and represent two sides of the same coin. What would it take to breathe into your fear and charge it with the passionate, driving force of excitement? The next time you're concerned with how someone will react when they read the words you've so painstakingly written, take a deep breath. Physically. Inhale fresh air. Let it fill every crevice of your lungs. Then breathe out. Repeat this deep breath three times as you think about that fear. Has there been any change? By physically introducing breath into your fear, how has the energy behind it shifted?

Maybe like me with some of my deepest, scariest moments, all you feel is a little less jittery. Which is awesome because that by itself is still progress. Other times you may get clarity or an insight that whispers to you, "You're worried about nothing," accompanied by a little flutter in the pit of your stomach. That flutter is the birth of the energy of excitement. Your fear... *with* the breath in it! By bursting through your fear (or in some cases tiptoeing around it), you're able to embrace your truth, your words, and your impact on your world.

BECAUSE... WORDS

Nothing changes the world quite like words. Words expressed verbally in conversation, in a progression of tones via song, words read to a child still in the womb or spoken to a plant in a science experiment... and of course, words written in a book. People can be convinced to sway their opinions through the passionate delivery of words. They can be led to action through words. They can even be led like cows to the slaughterhouse with—you guessed it—*words*. Words are the most powerful form of persuasion and manipulation that exists. Yehuda Berg said;

> Words are singularly the most powerful force available to humanity. We can choose to use this force constructively with words of encouragement, or destructively using words of despair. Words have energy and power with the ability to help, to heal, to hinder, to hurt, to harm, to humiliate, and to humble.

Wow. If words are *this* powerful, just imagine what *your* words can do for someone else. And what your words can do for your*self*. If you're reading this book, then you call yourself a writer. This power of the written word is your legacy. It's your torch to carry (and sometimes your cross to bear). It's your humble responsibility to use your gift to bestow a legacy—an immortal message—to the future of this world. You have the power to help, heal, hinder, hurt, harm, humiliate, and humble billions of people—from those currently inhabiting this planet to all the billions to come. Make your choice as to which of these you will impart.

This is a huge responsibility. A great power. Something to be feared, yes, but more than that, something to excite. So the next time you're faced with that fear of what others might think or how your writing will be judged, remember your responsibility. Your mission. Your power. And most of all, your written voice. You are the writer destined to change your world, one reader at a time.

So write with passion. Allow your truth to be your therapy. Breathe excitement into your fear. Use your words. Write your immortality.

BEING A WRITER BRINGS GREAT POWER.

ABOUT
KRISTEN JOY LAIDIG

Kristen Joy Laidig decided she was "unemployable" at the tender age of six when she started her first business making and selling pet rocks with nothing but a Sharpie® marker, gravel, and ingenuity. A serial entrepreneur, in 2003 she turned her life-long love of writing into a full-time career teaching authors and entrepreneurs how to create books that bring them business by founding the internationally-known brand, *The Book Ninja*®.

She has authored over 40 books, started over 50 publishing companies, trained over 10,000 authors worldwide, has her black belt in karate, and eats way too much chocolate.

She currently changes lives through her students... one published message at a time, manages her two retail stores *Toy Box Gifts & Wonder*® and *Nerdvana Outpost* in the heart of her newfound hometown, Chambersburg, PA, is in the start-up phase of at least three new businesses at any given time, and generally causes anyone reading this bio to be out of breath.

On her "off" time (what's that?) she brainstorms business ideas with her awesome husband, the great Public Domain Expert himself, Tony Laidig, and hangs out with her two ragdoll kitties. She's even been known to sleep... occasionally.

Visit KristenJoysBlog.com to learn more.

WRITING IS ART

Join our Free Community!

WritingIsArt.com

Made in the USA
Monee, IL
14 October 2021